Lightning Evolution of Humanity: rEvolution – Awakening

Volume 2

Socially-Economically-Political rEvolution [IMHO]

I. Disclosing the wrong, sick, Evil and enormously inequitable socially-economically-politically-environmental System of this world

II. Fixing the wrong aspects of the sick and Evil socially-economically-politically-spiritually-religiously-philosophical SYSTEM of this world as far as the social, economical and political factors and aspects are concerned. Reasons for the rEvolution, aims, outlines, strategies and solutions

III. Healing the hearts and minds socially-economically-spiritually-religiously-philosophically programmed and conditioned on Fear and Anxiety, greed, callousness towards suffering, obduracy, insensibility, passiveness and indifference to Evil

Rarely do we find men who willingly engage in hard, solid thinking. There is an almost universal quest for easy answers and half-baked solutions. Nothing pains some people more than having to think.

• Martin Luther King, Jr.

The table of contents

1. Preface

This book was originally one with the spiritually-religiously-philosophically-psychological aspects of the System and Lightning Evolution of Humanity, of which the book is meant to be an integral and valid part, but I decided to split the original version into two Volumes.. I encourage you to read Volume 1.. both Volumes underwent quite serious revisions in the process of splitting.. new ideas, new arguments..

This book is a simple partial solution to the inequitable, sick, socially-economically-politically-spiritually-psychologically-religiously-environmental System..

A significant part of the Volume 1 of the book is debunking of some wrong statements by renown people like Buddha, E. Tolle, Confucius, W. Dyer, Plato or Swindoll, etc.. Actually I like and respect them on the most but not BLINDLY – always with discerning eye however fancy their maxims are. They are but humans and Errare humanum est [It is human to err].. such claims residing in the consciousness of many - and thus fooling them and veiling the Truth, the REAL - establish this world, civilization, science, philosophy and I found out that quite many are wrong.. ERGO the foundations of the civilization are false.. so I am trying to change the situation.. If the foundations of the world are mediocre, then what kind of world is built on them? What kind of Humanity?

Do not believe in anything simply because you have heard it. Do not believe in traditions because they have been handed down for many generations. Do not believe anything because it is spoken and rumored by many. Do not believe in anything because it is written in your religious books. Do not believe in anything merely on the authority of your teachers and elders. But after observation and analysis, when you find that anything agrees with reason and is conducive to the good and the benefit of one and all, then accept it and live up to it. - Buddha

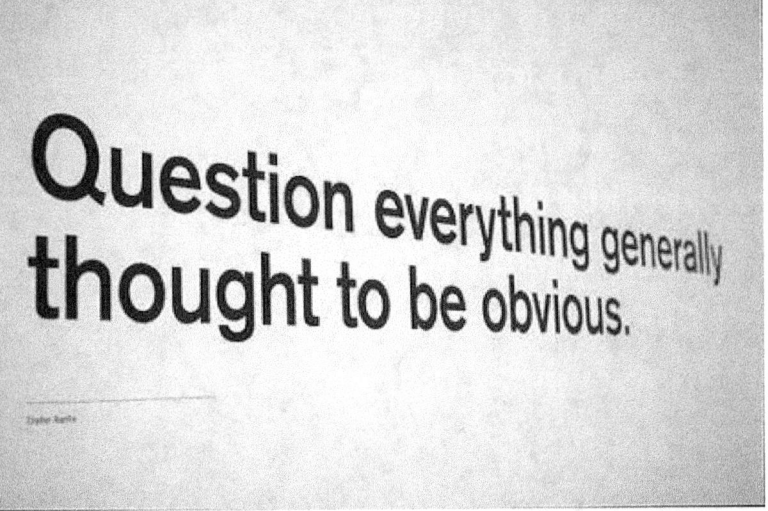

Most valid issue here is the sick socially-economically-politically-psychologically-spiritually-religious unjust, inequitable and unfair SYSTEM with its gargantuan economic gap between the incomes of the top richest people and the vast majority of the poor where 1.4Bil people live on less than $1 daily and suffer from hunger, every 5s a child dies from it, 2.8Bil People live in EXTREME poverty on less than $2 daily and some 6Bil+ people live in relative poverty while some maybe 1.5-2Bil over-consuming people programmed environmentally – and within that by media too – kill themselves to support their families and pay credits back – sometimes working 12-16h daily while 10h+ work a day is a probably standard for most of them. This is SLAVERY.

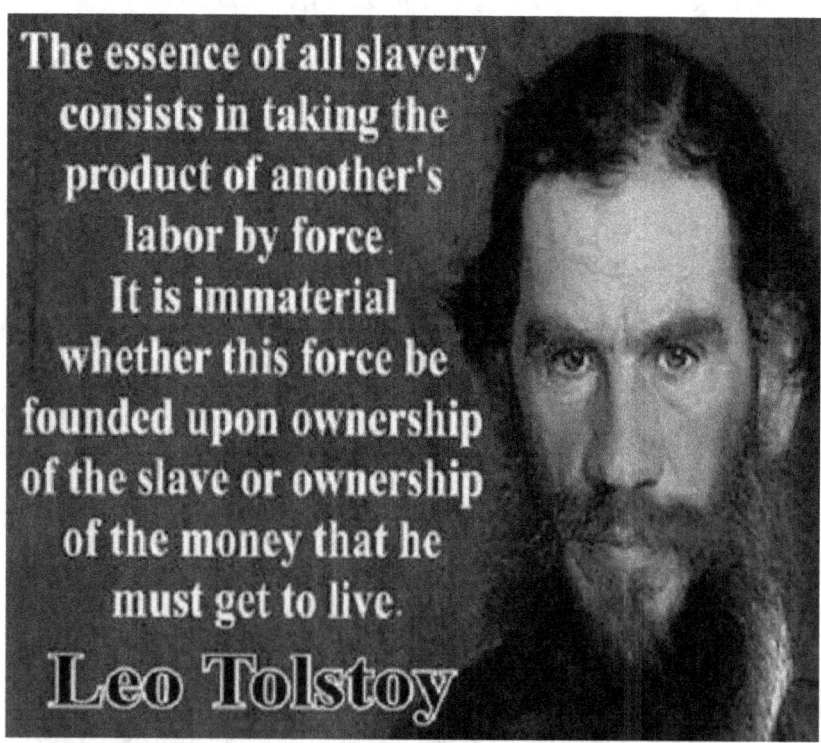

The essence of all slavery consists in taking the product of another's labor by force. It is immaterial whether this force be founded upon ownership of the slave or ownership of the money that he must get to live.
Leo Tolstoy

AND I present some POSSIBLE and EASILY EXECUTABLE solutions to this problem as long as the governments and the richest would co-operate, as well - which I am aware how unlikely it is right now BUT maybe

THIS book WILL change little SOMETHING about THAT.

I prove that this planet can EASILY afford decent life for EVERYONE! For instance the World Hunger total solution demands humble $30Bil a year – problem solved ENTIRELY. At the same time the Forbes TOP 1600+

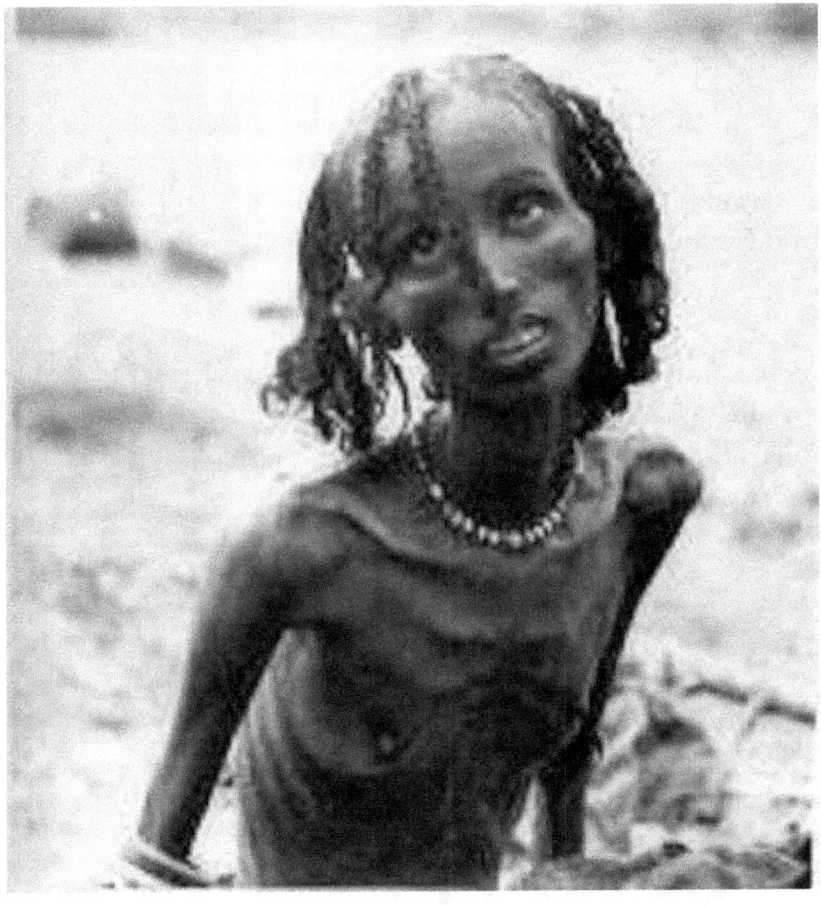

billionaires of the world could solve it alone with their aggregate wealth of $6.4Trillion of which 0.47% is the

$30Bil which is needed. BUT they don't give a fuck! :/ :(

>>> $30 billion per year is needed to end world hunger.

>>> $660 billion per year is the amount Congress spends on Defense.

http://borgenproject.org/the-cost-to-end-world-hunger/

Also I consider the role of English queen and England as a hypothetical Ruler Of The Planet and the Rothschild and Rockefeller Dynasties role.

The aspect of global wealth and income: The global Wealth by Credit Suisse is ca. $250Trillions and the top 1% wealthiest people have ½ of that – OFFICIALLY. But I found out that some of the richest are not listed on

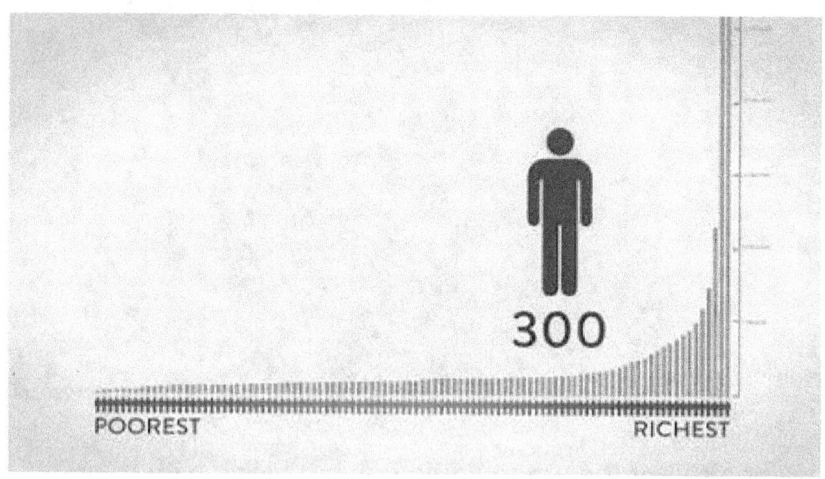

300

POOREST   RICHEST

Forbes World Billionaires List. So maybe they are not counted by Credit Suisse, either and the GW is for instance $555Trillions, not 250. If divided equally $250Trillions/7.15Billions people = $35'000 per capita [$105'000 per a standard family of 3] – be it a child, adult or an elderly person. If it is,say, $444Trillions then we get $62'097 per capita [$251'848 per a family of 4] for all people on Earth.. but maybe the REAL GW is much much more than the officially published one..

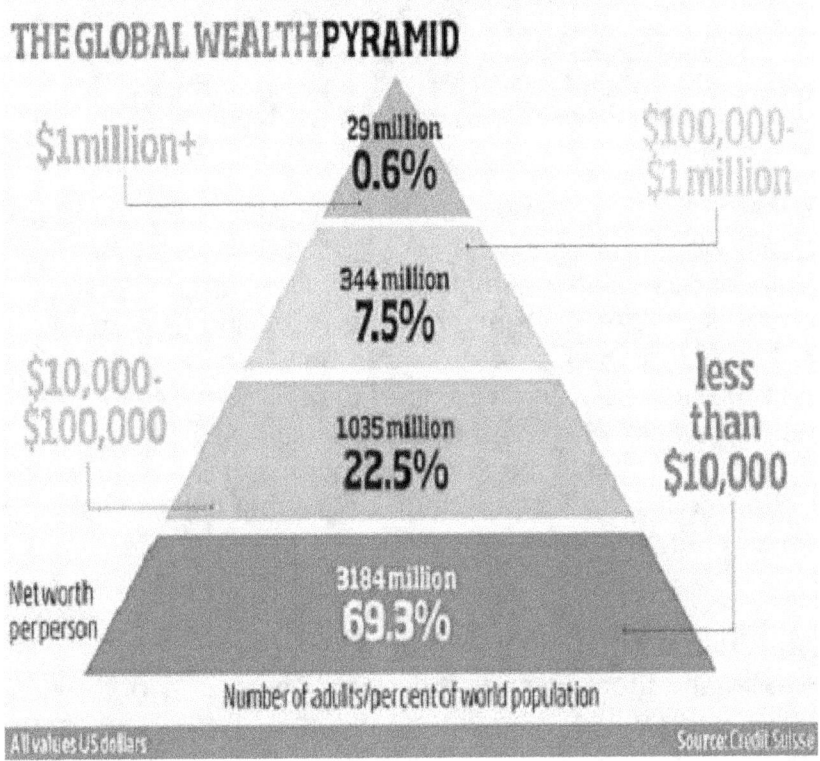

THE GLOBAL WEALTH PYRAMID

$1million+

29 million
0.6%

$100,000-
$1 million

344 million
7.5%

$10,000-
$100,000

1035 million
22.5%

less
than
$10,000

Net worth
per person

3184 million
69.3%

Number of adults/percent of world population

All values US dollars

Source: Credit Suisse

[2012 data above and below]

11

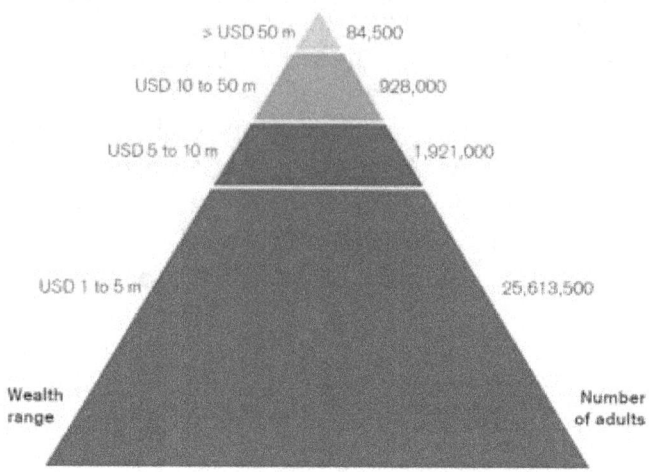

Source: James Davies, Rodrigo Lluberas and Anthony Shorrocks, Credit Suisse Global Wealth Databook 2012

> USD 50 m   84,500

USD 10 to 50 m   928,000

USD 5 to 10 m   1,921,000

USD 1 to 5 m   25,613,500

Wealth range   Number of adults

If the global income was shared equally EVERY standard family of 4 would get AT LEAST $33'000 annually [relevant calculations in chapter 4.], yet I am not saying that this EQUAL system would be FAIR and EQITABLE.. but I say that the gargantuan gap between the richest and the poorest must be limited to minimum. Maybe the below system where the richest get some twice+ more than the poorest is much better because it would provide better motivation for work than somewhat communist equal sharing..

As you look at the chart below relevant both for the wealth and the income you see that some 20% of the rich have and earn ca. 2 times that much as the poor except for ca. 5% of the richest and ca. 20% of the poorest.. In such system the higher incomes and wealth could be determined by employment because in fact only ca. 1/2 of the present labor force [3.1 billions people] is needed to provide production for the whole population.. thus the motivation for work would be sustained.. In fact the reason why so many enormously under-payed men work

is that they are cheaper than automation of ca. 1/2 of the global industry.. I was shocked when I learned that even tomatoes can be picked up automatically and that de facto it is cheaper and easier than human labor force..

True, real incomes and wealth are concealed by the rich and wealthiest for a whole variety of reasons: for instance to veil some of their gargantuan fortunes in order to avoid social unrests - this may happen either on small, individual scale or on a huge scale like country or global uprising or rEvolution].. the richest often keep their wealth in secrecy to avoid asking or begging for money, anger or robbing. It is quite obvious that most richest LIE about their money because they are afraid that 1 day people who were under-payed [robbed] by them in major ways will stand up for what really should be theirs. And take it.

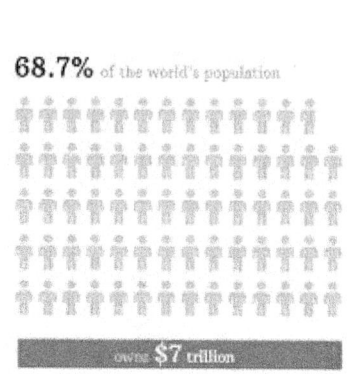

At present ca. 30 million richest people [0.42% of all humans] have the wealth of at least $1Mil totaling with their aggregate wealth at the volume of ca, $100Trillion [officially]. The Global Wealth 2013 by Credit Suisse was ca. $250Trillion [officially]. The conclusion is that the 30 million [0.42%] wealthiest men have the wealth equaling roughly the total aggregate wealth of the remaining 99.38% of all the people on Earth. Is this OK with you? Is this fair and equitable? To me this is EVIL. The sick socially-economically-politically-spiritually-psychologically-religious SYSTEM gives the 0.42% the POWER. And The System sustains such state of reality. [In fact I have very serious doubts about the Suisse Credit data correctness and validity and I think that they are misleading and the real Global Wealth is A WAY bigger and so is the gap between the wealthiest and the poor – The System's deception]

Now, ARE the 1.4Bil starving on less than $1 daily really fully responsible, GUILTY of their socially-economic status? Or the 2.8 living in EXTREME poverty? Or finally 6Bil+ living in relative poverty? Have they worked not hard enough or are not knowledgeable, intelligent, strong or smart enough to live decently? Well, even IF so then those who are REALLY strong SHOULD help them, no? IS it not obvious? Is it not the first thing about being HUMAN? I state that these people are on the most COMPLETELY INNOCENT of their poor status. Isn't a higher status a question of parent's money or LUCK in most cases?

YOU DON'T NEED A REASON TO HELP PEOPLE.

AAOR **Strong** **people** stand up FOR THEMSELVES. But the *STRONGEST* People STAND UP FOR OTHERS

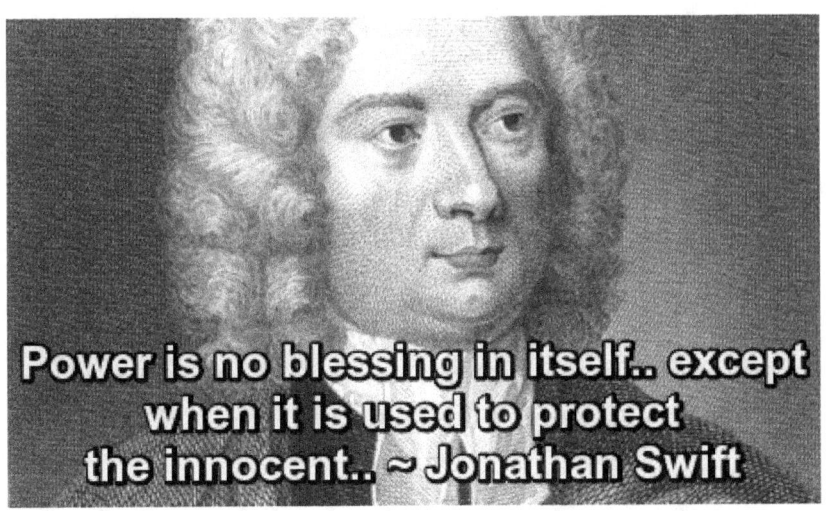

Power is no blessing in itself.. except when it is used to protect the innocent.. ~ Jonathan Swift

EVERYONE deserves decent life and this world CAN afford it – piece of cake – IF not the gargantuan INEQUITY, INEQUALITY and UNFAIRNESS and the horrendous gap between the incomes of the richest and the vast poor majority of the population.. I guess that you may easily comprehend my point here no matter what you were taught so far by some doubtful sources or "gurus" and if you only read the book with an open heart and mind. And I am not saying that ALL your sources or gurus are doubtful.. Some surely are not that much so and are fair and wise.. But the question remains: WHICH ONES?

The book mostly bases on the materials I published on Facebook during some last 3-4 years – my notes, the descriptions of text pictures, and often simply my expanded comments when I responded to people as exhaustively as I considered was necessary – despite

what numerous folks think about my "speeches". ;)
Because often speaking the full truth simply CANNOT be
limited to 1 or 2 eye-catching, witty sentences.. as you
may guess I was often unreasonably criticized for "too
long" comments and texts – NOW you have the
BOOK. :P

I believe that this book [as well as the Volume 1 of it
concerning the spiritually-religiously-philosophically-
psychological aspect of the sick, Evil and enormously
inequitable System of this planet] will change humanity
and the world IF only I menage to make some 50-250
thousands people read it..

Everything here [except most graphics and some
wikipedia stuff] is my own creation based on my
thoughts, feelings, suspicions and observations and
reads and some graphics, movies and music, too.

That all as well as Facebook and real life interactions
have been my increasing inspirations – particularly for
last few years until now I decided that I do not need to be
more ready and prepared to write it and that it just can
and should be done now.

Having almost all data made up the very process of
writing took me literally 4 days – right now I am ultimately
polishing the text and splitting the original one volume
book into two standalone Volumes: this one – the
socially-economically-politically-environmental aspects of
the System and the religiously-spiritually-philosophically-
psychological ones [done already] and this is 1st
September, 2014.

The book is often provocative, seditious and rebellious BUT I do not offer my DIVINE REVELATION INDISPUTABLE TRUTH here like many self-styled guru-types oh-so-damn-sure of everything they say or maybe rather pretending that they are right in everything. . Far from it. On the most I rather seed the doubts than dispel them. It is simply humanly impossible that I am always right here. The book is rather meant as a common ground and a starting point for a sort of debate over the issues which I move here. Also the texts were written in different times [different ages to me] and in different moods and with different attitudes so some are very emotional, sometimes a little angry or aggressive, sometimes maybe joyful or sometimes little sad.. I re-edited some most aggressive parts so the people take them easier but SOME words DO witness my anger because:

[Righteous – I] Anger is a gift – Malcolm X

Righteous Anger is the one which maybe characterizes the Archangels with flaming swords or maybe gods and some of you when you see persecution, injustice, extreme violence or inequity – Evil in one word – as I see that and it sometimes touches me and makes me cry without tears and sometimes it just PISSES ME OFF! O:-/

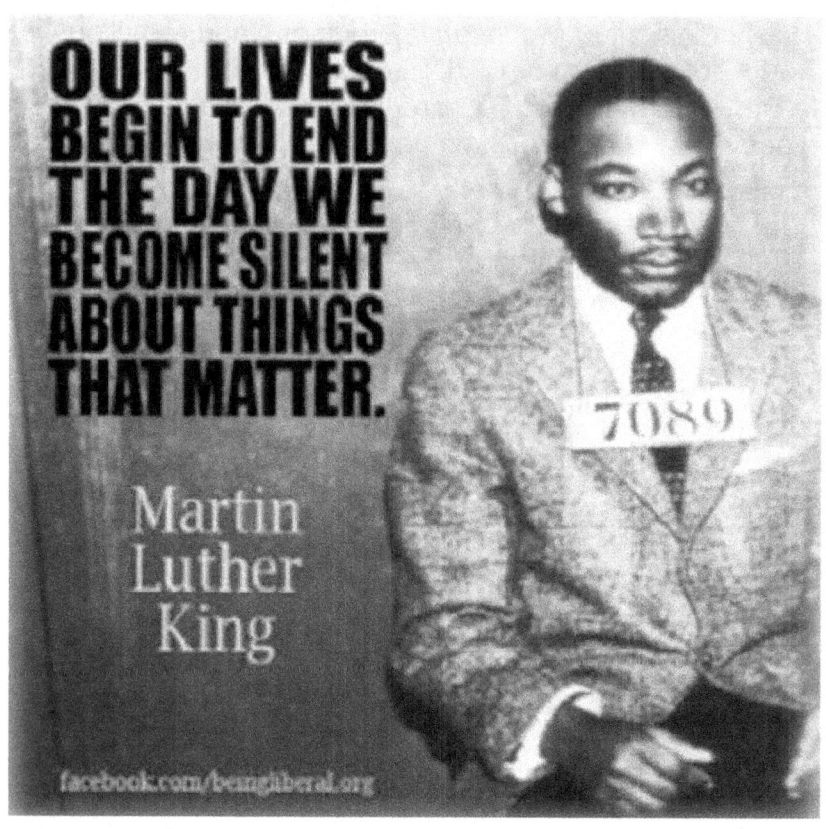

OUR LIVES BEGIN TO END THE DAY WE BECOME SILENT ABOUT THINGS THAT MATTER.

Martin Luther King

facebook.com/beingliberal.org

Exponentially shrinking numbers of increasingly enlightened people are deemed insane by exponentially increasing masses of decreasingly enlightened people. - xlivescom

I use lots of quotes here which I found and learned through years and which I consider the wisest of those I have spotted: I assimilated them as my own words after careful consideration.. still I have some doubts about some [especially when I quote myself ;) lol! :D 8| 8] :P] but even those in general are not THAT bad or stupid I think ;) :D

My writing is not free from presupposition [and obviously presumption] and I do admit it within it not only by using the abbreviation "imho" quite a few times [and especially in title of the book :D].. Sometimes you will find purposeful repetition or even contradiction here .. It is a mix of my opinions and facts [even here I am not fully sure of the sources] and I never deny it nor I present this sick attitude of "PAN-knowers" and alpha'n'omegas who hear something from their doubtful gurus/masters/leaders/preachers or read it in their holy books or in some of all those short maxims spread on the Web with pretty, shiny, colorful pictures or pretty movies on youtube and then: Satori! Awakening! Enlightenment! Mount Everest! Eureka! Out of the blue!

OR worse: just a plain desire to become a GURU – so in both cases they state it as a fact to their audience [the flock of stupid and naive sheep who blindly follow those kinds – the "Leaders"&"Masters"&"PAN-knowers"] and then all together they repeat wrong, stupid, short, eye-catching maxims blindly among each other [until they become popular and accepted "truths"] and almost nobody even ATTEMPTS to put them into question! BECAUSE THEY WERE TOLD SO BY THEY GURU/MASTERS – this is enough for a reason/evidence for the SHEEP! [here I am just a little pissed off at their unmeasurable, naive and blind stupidity O:-/] :P

SO DAMN SURE OF THEIR UNQUESTIONABLE ENLIGHTENED REVELATION!

AND HOW THEY GET MAD AND ANGRY WHEN YOU SAY THAT THEY ARE WRONG IN MOST PART - defending the chains they revere so much for any cost blindly and rejecting any use of reason [the chains – revered convictions deeply rooted in their consciousness and minds] – cognitive dissonance. And YET too LAZY to READ even 444 WORDS rejecting and/or denying their deeply rooted wrong convictions!

Myths which are believed in tend to become true. - George Orwell - Dangerous perspective but maybe he meant rather that those myths become True in the consciousness of the masses.. IMHO!

Almost all graphics in PDF are in High Resolution so if the texts, letters within them are too small you may zoom to read them..

You may wanna click on the below link to go directly to my Facebook which is open to public as most my FB materials are. I am an open source so if you wanna steal my stuff, be my guest and do not be shy – you are welcome and have a good theft :D <3 O:) 8| !

www.facebook.com/lukasz.czepulkowski444

I created a youtube playlist with 37 great, inspirational, mostly restful songs this night. I have exactly the same playlist on my Winamp :D and I am listening to it right now in random play mode. :D You may wish to listen to it while reading my books or whenever :D

But after converting to PDF the link to the playlist had all capital letters converted to small and did not work so you need to go to my channel [link below] and choose the playlist titled: "37 Inspirational Songs: Mostly Restful, Celtic Or Epic Ones.." [probably on the top]:

https://www.youtube.com/user/GabrielRainbows/playlists

Important: As long as their works are somehow connected with the wide, general idea of my writing, I will appreciate any serious offer of co-operation with persons who would be willing to add their materials to this book OR maybe the next which I will write. Their names would be mentioned as co-authors and they will participate in profits. ALSO I am open for any offer which would concern publishing the hard copy of this book for a modest price or selling the copyrights.

Since 01.01.2015 there is FREE download of the book provided on my website. Most probably this book will be sort of Live, anyway – the contents may be subject to change and maybe later in time I will add a few chapters. Eventual upgrades: the idea is that you just check my website from time to time to see for changes:

http://lightningevolution.wix.com/humanity-evolution

No pop-up windows, no registration needed, no hidden costs, no ads, no expensive paid SMS, no real personal data and no credit card data required nor any shitte like that on my site. EVER. The website is ready but I am still working on it.. As you see I can afford you to get the PDF or ePUB versions of the book for FREE there but the Kindle eBook on Amazon is some minimum money [$2-3 or free] - and the paperback version is obviously some modest money [depends on the eventual publisher] – as for now it is available on Amazon and some other associated online and offline bookstores for about $10-11 so maybe I will have some income because right now I have none.. As you see my main concern here is not so much profit but the numbers of readers who can afford the book as cheap as possible..

There is a space for comments in a form of a Forum on the website. Though the website PDF and ePUB formats of the book is free, if after reading anyone considers it a good job and worth some change cash and wants and is able to donate me even $1.44 I will be happy :) And if he sends me 3.14 or 4.44 dollars or more then I will be extremely happy because I have been broke for years now. The PayPal Donations buttons are provided in the website..

E-mail, PayPal: arcturian.dragon@yahoo.com

My bank account number for international cross-border transfers [4 big cash]:

IBAN: PL 03 1020 5402 0000 0002 0315 8714

SWIFT: BPKOPLPW

I plan creating a foundation aimed to feed some of 1.4Billion people suffering from World Hunger and kids dying from hunger every 5 seconds :-/ :-(<3

DISCLAIMER: As for the Forbes List 1600+ World billionaires – each of you must pay me $37'216'999.44 to be allowed by me to read this book. Seriously. I will use the money wisely and compassionately to help the weak. If you do not comply you will be doomed and go to HELL. God and the High Archangels' Council agreed with me in that by ACCLAMATION. O:-| -_- O:-|

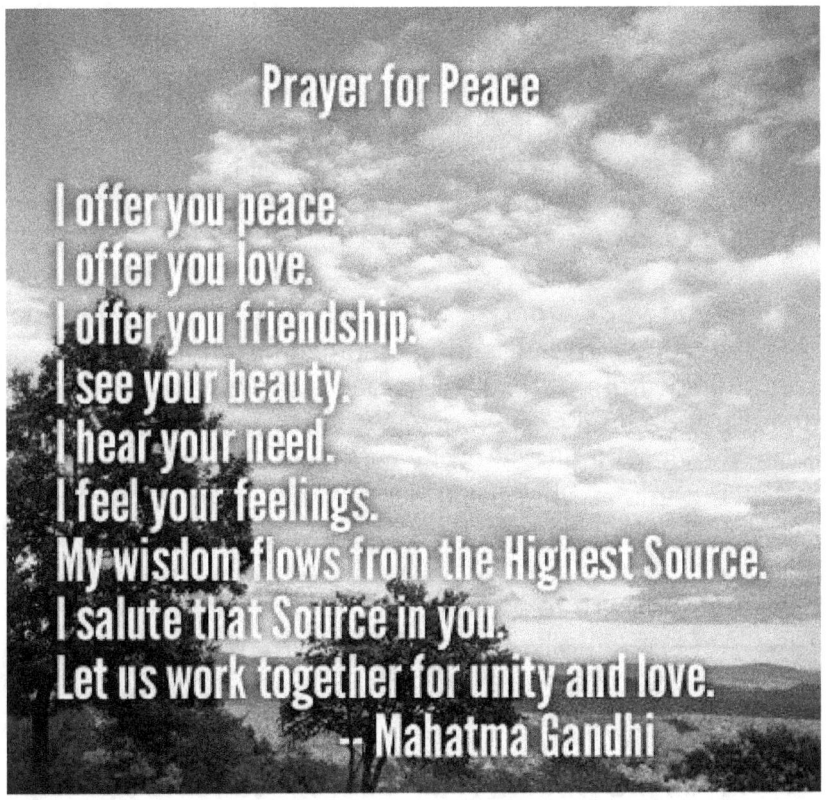

Prayer for Peace

I offer you peace.
I offer you love.
I offer you friendship.
I see your beauty.
I hear your need.
I feel your feelings.
My wisdom flows from the Highest Source.
I salute that Source in you.
Let us work together for unity and love.
-- Mahatma Gandhi

Few things you should really know about me: On the most I see things: the Cosmos and World with humans and maybe some entities out of this world as the widest spectrum of possibilities and probabilities and when I do not know I would partially assume the most probable working variant but I am always ready to rethink and change my mind if evidenced otherwise. I do not reject or approve any of them if not 100% sharp sure that they are 100% sharp real. And then I know something but in fact I know only a little. Some wise man said: "I know that I know nothing" and I say: "I know that I know a little". Who is more right? Who speaks the truth?

Maybe he really knew nothing and spoke the truth but maybe he only thought so humbly – especially that saying that he confirmed that he knew at least that particular one thing he said – a paradox. Or he was not sure if he spoke truth.. :)

And maybe I am wrong in what I wrote and in fact this is only my slightly megalomaniac conviction that I know something.. I am not sure. Maybe I should rethink-refeel and repeat exactly his words? I am aware that just a few lines above I admitted that I was sure 100% of some things but this is what the fusion of heart-mind I use to think~feel tells me.. but is it REAL? Maybe I should have said "I do not reject or approve any of them if not 99.9% sure that they are real." to leave a 0.1% gateway just in case that I am totally wrong? Man, I am not even sure if I exist myself.. if I am real..

..:Tell me what IS real. - Morpheus to Neo :..

I question, doubt and do not reject any of the abundance of possibilities which I see – I only see that some of them are more and some less probable and loosely hold on to the first while always ready to change my views – also I am wrong sometimes, maybe even often BUT again at least I seed the doubts where you are too sure without proper evidence while I am not and I dispel doubts when I am convinced that I see the truth – and I ALMOST NEVER lie – I put really lot of effort in not lying nor erring.. I am a Dragons' and Angels' Lover.. I would love the mighty, wise and Good-aligned Dragons to come over and fly in the skies everywhere along with Archangels with their flaming swords.. This world would change to Good one in a heartbeat then.. I wish..Then so be it..

Fly High, Family!

DIGRESSION:

WE ARE READY FOR THE LIGHTNING EVOLUTION OF HUMANITY [AND THE PLANET] = (R)EVOLUTION!

First duty of a modern Warrior, Knight of Freedom, Truth, Equity, Love, Honor and Valor is to protect the innocent and weak [like poor] persecuted by the SYSTEM.

"A sword is not meant to kill but to protect that which matters most."

I am convinced that the first ambitious, very well justifiable, most equitable and honorable and extremely valid and noble task of grand valor, courage and virtue for The rEvolution People is to provide the food for every kid dying from hunger every 5s.. 1.4 people suffering from World Hunger and aid for 2.8billions people living in EXTREME poverty on less than $2 daily.. JUST THIS.. let's make the RICHEST, WEALTHIEST pay for the food..

ONLY $30billions annually is needed to solve the World Hunger problem entirely.. 1.5% of what goes on military in the world.. and if only the 250 millions richest men gave $10 a month for this cause then the problem is SOLVED.. **The 1600+ world billionaires list totals aggregate $6.4 trillions of which $30 billions is barely 0.47%! let's MAKE them GIVE a damn!** Piquets, marches, demonstrations.. gatherings.. free media.. peaceful solution.. this CAN be done and if THIS is DONE then we have our FIRST HUGE V*I*C*T*O*R*Y! Then we DO know that we have THE POWER and can go further.. and WIN.. the second battle is for the 2.8bilions in extreme poverty.. this is not much more expensive for the wealthiest than the entire eradication of World Hunger.. and then NEXT.. we decide later.. I have many ideas almost ready.. we will go ALL THE WAY

P*E*A*C*E*F*U*L*L*Y but imminently! THEY.. the Shadow Elite.. **The rulers and masters of this world of slaves WILL finally YIELD after 1000s years!**

And please spare yourself the empty talks that they HONESTLY earned their wealth [reducing the wages and stealing LIVES because billions under-payed men have to work their assess off to make up for their families for anything close to decent livelihood] Please spare empty talks about the FUCKING FISHING RODS for the poor so they make up for living by them selves.. 1000s kids in agony.. YOU wanna give them the RODS???

Better shove them up your smart-differently asses!
Besides, you don't give them away, anyway!

When you see a victim of a car accident in agony do you
give him a syringe, band-aids, medicines and
resuscitation kits for self-service?? yes? I bet that for
more reasonable people this is enough for an initial
argument, reason, evidence that the 2 steps I mention
here are vital while half of the food in USA goes to
garbage and cows in EU are subsided more money than
$2 daily which 2.8billions people live on and the dear
money spent unnecessarily on pet food is more than
needed to save the lives of billions human beings!

The next step imho should be making the elites.. government to establish the MAXIMUM wages and MAXIMIZE the minimum wages so 6Bil+ under-payed poor [relatively] people are payed accordingly to the REAL worth of their work and can work less [4-5h daily] to provide decent life for their families with less effort and are better motivated and come back home after work with still some energy left for taking care for instance for their self-development.. The surplus of the production and income over the maximum wage would provide minimizing the economic gap between the poorest and the wealthiest in a form of something like tax..

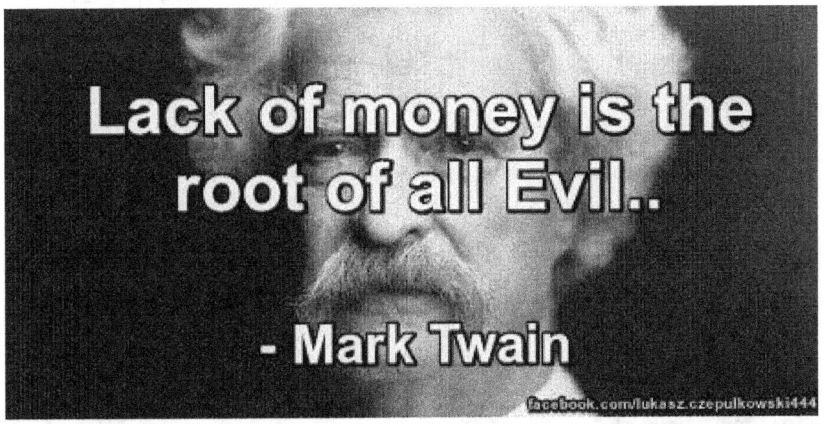

I am not sure if Twain and Shaw really said that [because very often fake, and/or untrue words are put in the mouths of certain authorities in the Web] and rather not ALL Evil BUT nonetheless, these words express a lot of Truth.. certainly if all the poor in the world had enough money for modest but decent livelihood the world would be a lot better place to live in and Humanity would be a way happier because Fear and anxiety about the future

33

would be eradicated at least as economical aspects are involved and that would be a lot.. thus there would be much less anger, envy, aggression or hatred left and a way less conflicts - military conflicts about the resources included.. besides people would have more time for mentally-spiritual self-development which would greatly improve the quality of the whole Humanity..

On the other hand it is said that "Money is the root of all Evil" which only seemingly contradicts the first claim because the reason why is that money is distributed extremely unfairly and inequitably and if it was different, then it would not induce too much Evil, however, maybe the world would be the best place to live in, if there was no money at all because in fact it is maybe redundant.. but before that should happen we must work on the proper wealth distribution in form of money..

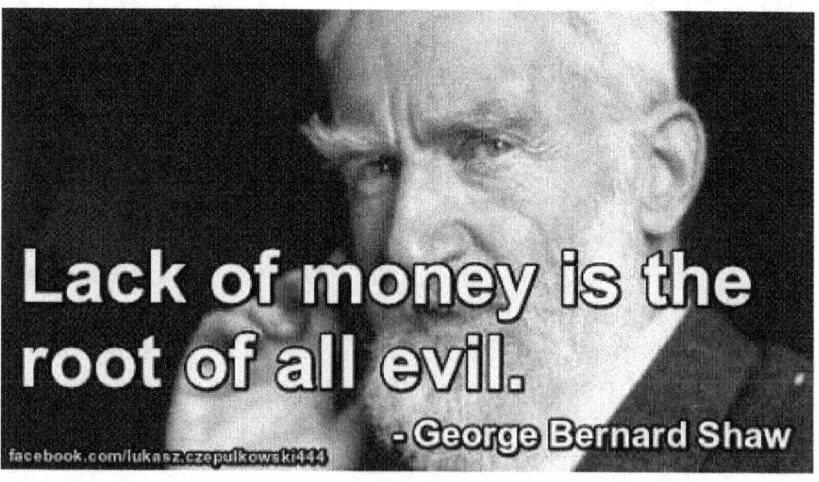

Lack of money is the root of all evil.

- George Bernard Shaw

facebook.com/lukasz.czepulkowski444

Also I guess that the root of the problem is Fear and

anxiety and the lack of True Love [especially in the most of the wealthiest people] which they exclude.. if the richest and most powerful knew Love they would obviously stand up for the poor and weak and share their vast wealth fairly.. I am developing the problem of wealth and incomes inequality and injustice more exhaustively especially in chapters 3. and 4. of this book..

And lastly, it is quite commonly considered that most poor people are better than most rich people, according to which lack of money brings about no Evil and quite the opposite but here I say that the situation in which the vast majority of good people are poor is Evil by itself and evoked, induced and maintained by the very narrow group -oligarchy - of the most rich and powerful men who fully control the world wealth and income distribution and sustain the status quo of this monstrously unjust , wrong, sick, Evil and inequitable System of the modern world..

2. Gargantuan socially-economical inequality of this world.. a set of vital facts..

$30Bil is needed to eradicate the World Hunger This is what the world spends in 8 days on military: 1.7% of the annual military expenditures.

The assets of the world's three richest men exceed the combined Gross Domestic Products of the world's 48 poorest countries. - Web

The world has enough for everyone's need but not enough for everyone's GREED. - a man with a poster in the street [USA]

Every 5s a child dies from hunger.. 6 millions kids annually. - Mathematics

12Mil people annually die from hunger. - Mathematics

Over 6Bil people live in relative poverty and some 1-1.5Bil over-consuming people also kill themselves to feed their families and pay credits, many often working 12-14h daily. - Web

It's been proven that the wealthiest nations do not have the healthiest people – they live in the countries where the smallest economic gap between the rich and poor.

100 richest men in the world have a total wealth of more than $2Trillion, roughly equaling the annual income of the half of the humanity [the poorest half].

1.4Bil of them live on less than $1 daily.

2.8Bil people live on less than $2 a day

Every cow in the European Union is subsidized $2.50 a day.

Global Military expenditures are ca. $1.7Trillion

The amount of money spent on pet food in the US and EU annually equals the additional amount needed to provide basic food and health care for All the people in the poor countries with a sizable amount left over.

Nearly ½ of the food America produces is WASTED.

In 2005 over 7 million people were under some form of correctional supervision or in prison. In 1980 it would have been less than 2 million. Are today 15-20 millions in prisons? Why?

There are over 67'000 people employed in the lobbying industry in Washington DC – 125 for each elected congressman.

Almost 2/3 of all US companies paid NO TAX between 1996-2000.

6 million children die from hunger each year-every time you take a breath, another child in a poor country dies from hunger-related causes.

By this time tomorrow, 18,000 more children will have died unnecessarily of hunger. Looks like maybe HIGHEST time for the richest ones to S H A R E finally and entirely change the present socially-economically-politically-religiously-spiritual SYSTEM?

Almost half of the world's wealth is now owned by just one percent of the population.

The wealth of the one percent richest people in the world officially amounts to ca. $110 trillion. That's 65 times the total wealth of the bottom half of the world's population.

The bottom half of the world's population owns the same as the richest 85 people in the world officially.

Seven out of ten people live in countries where economic inequality has increased in the last 30 years.

During the Age of Reason, Francis Bacon wrote *"Above all things good policy is to be used so that the treasures and monies in a state be not gathered into a few hands... Money is like fertilizer, not good except it be spread."*

Estimates suggest that the lower half of the global population possesses barely 1% of global wealth, while the richest 10% of adults own 86% of all wealth, and the top 1% account for 46% of the total.

The top 400 Americans have more wealth than lower half of all Americans combined.

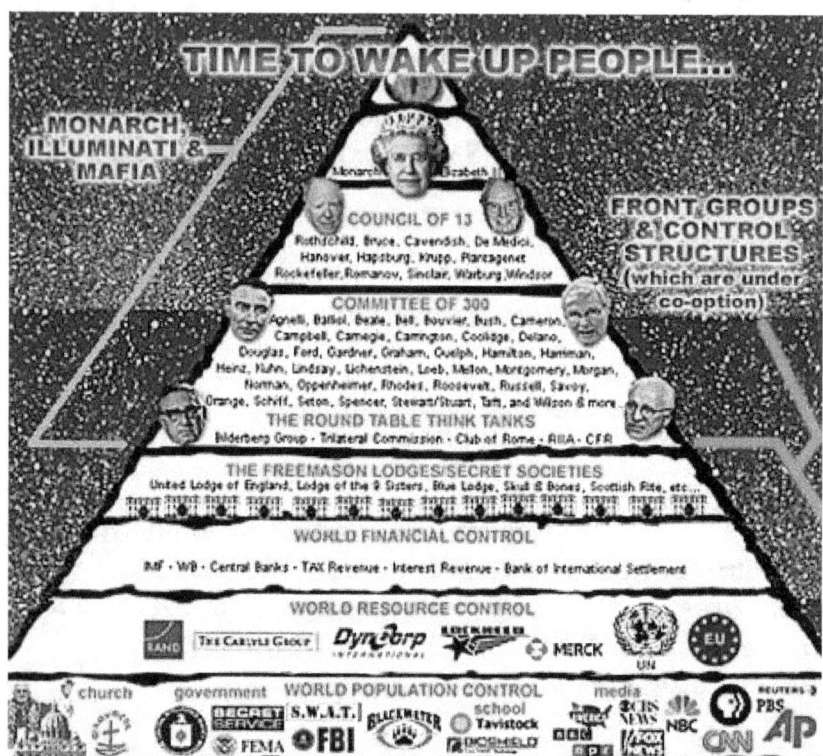

3. HOW CAN THE THE RICHEST PEOPLE LIVE AND SLEEP PEACEFULLY KNOWING THAT EVERY 5s A CHILD DIES FROM HUNGER? Don't they know that they die? THEN TELL THEM!

This chapter does not concern ONLY Angelina Jolie family BUT they are the best working example for me to go through first to state my point clearly so let me start here:

While searching for the amounts of money spent by the couple on charity I found some $25Mil spent by Angie and Brad personally between 2006 and 2009 – this is not nothing but still a drop in the sea compared to their official total wealth of $340Mil [+/ - 7% of it]. If they have donated similar money from 2010 until now then the total now should be some $50Mil.. which is maybe good enough for them but not for me.. especially that I found no donations made by them to the people starving from hunger and dying from it except maybe $1Mil for Doctors Without Borders who logically must feed their patients, too..

BUT Oprah Winfrey Is said to be the Most Generous Celeb, Donating $41 Million to Charity, so Pitts most probably gave away less than that..

I am not sure of this data and sources because Brad and Angie have few foundations which are financed by other people except themselves, as well, so maybe in fact they gave less for charity. Also I consider that they should support the starving people with food first of all as a priority and not give money first for other purposes like they do. The most evident example is Brad's $16Mil given to rebuild storm struck New Orleans [it is by his foundation "Make it Right" financed by some more people than just him]. Well, to me you did not '"make it right'", Brad, because first of all you should save the kids dying every 5s.. homelessness is still not DEATH..

Another extremely valid issue here are the charitable contribution deductions. In case of the Jolie-Pitts the income tax in 2013 was 39.6% which percentage of their donations [at least] they deduct from their tax. In other words every time they donated $5Mil then IN FACT they spent only $3Mil – at most, because with their top top lawyers and counselors MOST probably they can save much more than $2Mil on each $5Mil charity donation.. So MOST probably between 2006-2014 they spend NOT $50Mil on charity BUT maximum $30Mil. Which is still a lot IF not the cherry on the cake:

The Pitts are said to spend $10Mil annually on their kids! Shame on you [unless the source is wrong]! This would be enough for your whole family to live happily for 100 years with everything provided that is needed or to save thousands kids from starving to DEATH!

Therefore I cannot say that the couple do nothing about the wrongs of this world but imho they often help in the wrong fields first of all and secondly: C'mmon! EVERYONE expects such people to give something to charity! So they just play their social role well! This is more or less about the publicity. They are thus more popular and make more money. Of course I cannot deny them SOME humanitarian impulses but is this simply kindness and compassion? Maybe it is feeding their egos via giving the offal of their abundant table to a variety of the needing ones: "Now I am so altruistic, kind and I help people so much, damn I am so glorious!" Or maybe I am wrong.

They are such hypocrites.. that couple Jolie and Pitt with their +/- $340Mil.. why they do not give 90% of that to the hungry children dying every 5s.. Is $34Mil left not enough for even a big family of 10 members to live very well for over 100 years? Which family really NEEDS SUCH money and those castles? For WHAT? Just GREED that spoiled the men' souls.. Well, she was in Iraq and Africa.. they adopted some black kids, too.. most of all for PUBLICITY as it seems? HOW much did they GIVE to the POOREST, HUNGRY people, children actually, truly? How many lives they DID save actually? So do they REALLY help a lot those who need help the most? She and Brad can afford to give away almost all money they have - $330Mil – and STILL live happily ever after for the $10Mil left! Oh Damn them.. let them keep even 30$Mil!

I am sure that even the "MODEST" $10Mil is a way more

than enough for EVERYTHING for even such a dear family like Pitts, Cruises [Tom], De Niros or Depps for 50 years - $166'666.66 a year: good schools, insurances, decent clothes, food and decent cars and a even a semi-luxury house and few simple apartments for the grown-up children and bills and some traveling around the world – DAMN! EVEN a decent 10 seats airplane for gods' sake! - EVEN if NONE of them worked for money for 50 years BUT this certainly would NOT be the case because they would work and more big money would flow to them.. must there be few CASTLES like theirs? Like the one in Spain or France in the photo? GREED spoiled the men' souls.. and it is so EVIL. Many say oh-so-wisely "Instead of giving a fish give the poor the fishing rod so he learns how to gain food and can do it by himself" Really..

Would you give a scalpel, band-aid, syringe and disinfectant to the heavily wounded so he treats him himself? So then would you give that rod to the kid dying [agony] from hunger with the same logic? If yes then you are like stupid and stone-hearted multimillionaires like Pitt, Gibson, Nicholson, de Niro, Van Damme, Stallone, Schwarzeneger, Rihanna, Madonna, Pavarotti and Depp [they have $100s millions] who would repeat this bullshit as rich man used to do [unless of course they use their money for the poorest in secret and I have not not heard about it – but my good guess is they DON'T or they give TOO little or for wrong, secondary causes – or sometimes they are just poor, crazy drugs and alcohol doing brokes – then cure them and help them, too]

Sooo.. WHO ARE THESE PEOPLE?!?

I persist strongly that feeding those who die from hunger every second is THE INDISPUTABLE PRIORITY in CHARITY and who does not see it is just an IDIOT! Of course later, AFTER they feed the dying from HUNGER, they SHOULD give them those FISHING RODS which on the most they DO NOT, either, only TALKING about it instead!

The Pitts were voted the most beautiful people in the world once a few years ago by some magazine I guess.. nothing more misleading.. they are only PRETTY and NOT beautiful.. beauty is in the heart even if the face is ugly.. Those all "TOP CLASS, TOP STARS" people on the most are ONLY PRETTY and not BEAUTIFUL.. they ACT.. they PLAY.. PRETENDERS.. Another thing is that often these pretties lives are much easier than the rest have..

The complete solution for the World Hunger is just BUT $30Bil a year.. I am not saying that Jolie, Pitt, Deep, De Niro, Willis, Rihanna, Madonna, U2, Rolling Stones, Beyonce, Katy Perry and the rest of the "TOP" stars who have $100s millions can solve or should solve the problem alone [though they could in fact for few years and still leave those $10-20Mil each for themselves] but the members of upper-medium and higher classes can easily afford to give some $10 a month for that purpose which is a way more than enough.

The clue is HOW to MAKE them life[money]-thieves to do that. I think that the whole problem here is just greed, stupidity and stone hearts. Here is the math: top rich 250'000'000 people give away $10/month=$120/year >>> $30Bil/year. What's TEN BUCKS for them? Voila! World Hunger problem solved!

You may replace "AFRAID" in the picture with "SHY"

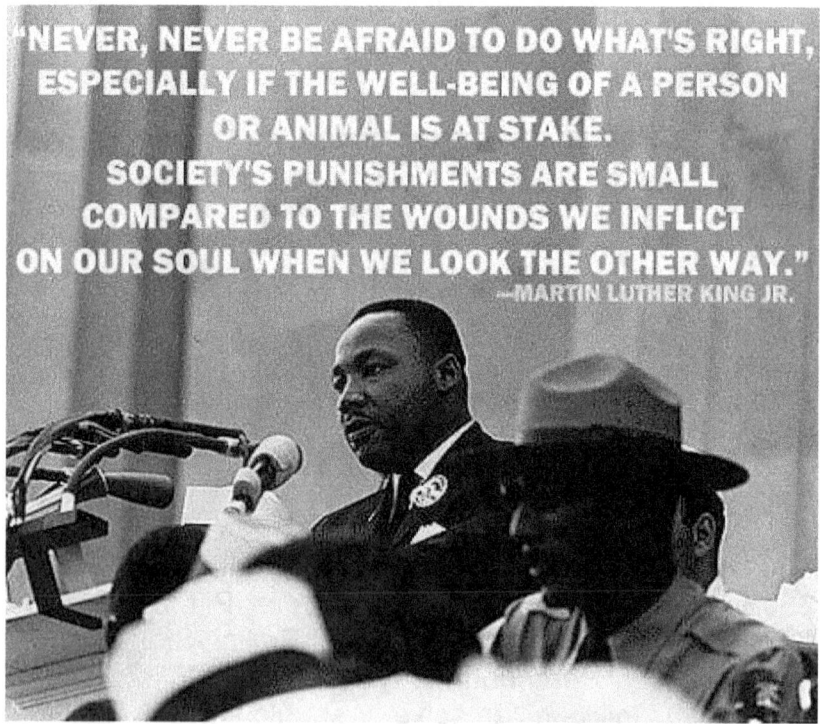

"NEVER, NEVER BE AFRAID TO DO WHAT'S RIGHT, ESPECIALLY IF THE WELL-BEING OF A PERSON OR ANIMAL IS AT STAKE. SOCIETY'S PUNISHMENTS ARE SMALL COMPARED TO THE WOUNDS WE INFLICT ON OUR SOUL WHEN WE LOOK THE OTHER WAY."
—MARTIN LUTHER KING JR.

I know many say "they earned their money with hard and

honest work" But why a McDonald worker earns 1000s times less than some CEOs.. or a simple construction worker and a top-top STAR? IS it REALLY only their "HARD AND HONEST" work what counts for such gargantuan wages? Well maybe sometimes it is.. maybe even often.. but does it still mean that they have to earn 10x.. 100x.. 1000x more than others whose work is also hard and honest?

Are the rich really working 100s or 1000s times more or are 100s or 1000s times smarter or wiser or more intelligent and efficient and deserve their sick money 10s, 100s or 1000s times more? Do I make some sense to you here? Imho the gap between the highest and the lowest income should be regulated at a much lower volume via setting maximum wage as it is with minimum wage and this could and should be done by the country, government..

Imagine just Bill Gates alone with his $70Bil wealth and yearly income at the tens or most probably hundreds millions if not few billions and the maximum wage set at $1Mil.. or 3 or 5Mil – I am sure enough for more than good life – and his surplus labor money – hundreds millions go to the poorest so the average world income is balanced more fairly. As easy as that and the maximum wages would allow this to happen.. and I well guess that the world minimum yearly income then could be set at over $10'000 per capita. Damn! Even if 7'000 then we ALL are good ever since economically! This is about FREEDOM! And I hope this is the close Future.. The present System is very unjust and EVIL!

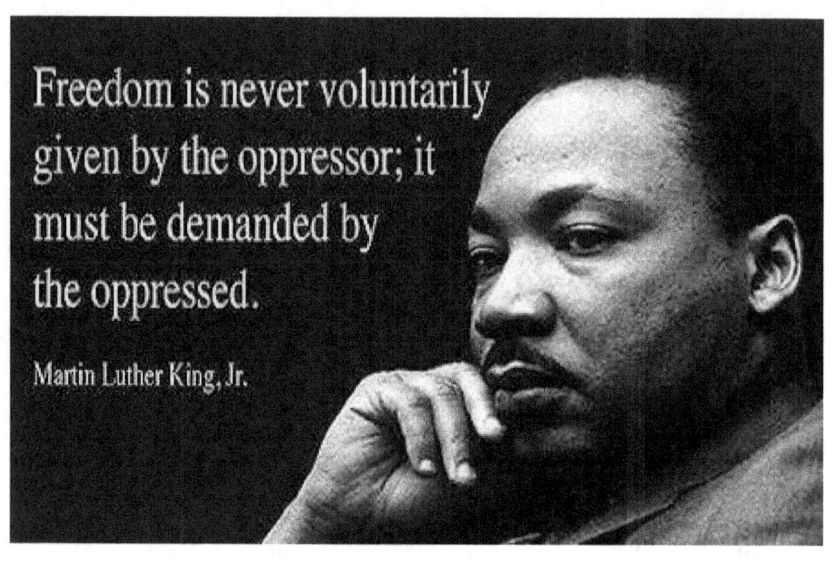

Freedom is never voluntarily given by the oppressor; it must be demanded by the oppressed.

Martin Luther King, Jr.

In the meantime in Uruguay: Ecce Homo!

THE POOREST PRESIDENT IN THE WORLD

PRESIDENT OF URUGUAY JOSÉ MUJICA DONATES 90% OF HIS $12,500 SALARY TO CHARITY AND KEEPS ONLY $1,250

And HERE I see the role of the top stars of the entertainment industry: They are FAMOUS.. their words and deeds count for lots of people.. they are often examples to follow for others.. authorities.. now imagine WHAT IF some most rich and famous stars gave away half or more of their fortunes to feed the 1.4Bil starving people? This would be the cover story in most papers for years and news on TV.. Example to follow for the flock of sheep..

And then WHAT IF via becoming these examples and way-showers for them they convinced the upper-medium and higher classes to actually GIVE AWAY those FUCKING TEN BUCKS A MONTH to solve the World Hunger problem entirely.. And finally WHAT IF this all made the REALLY richest [Rothschild, Warburg, Morgan, Hapsburg, Rockefeller, Gates, Buffet..] and multi-billionaires.. maybe even few Trillionaires in hide who we even have not ever heard of and who REALLY OWN this whole PLANET – many of the the richest are NOT even on the Forbes List though the top 1600+ World's billionaires could probably buy off the half of Earth with their aggregate wealth of $6.4Trillion – I mean that they alone can control the planet and to control means to HAVE it – I want them to share with the poorest – really few men.. 1% of 1% of 1% - the oligarchy who own the 99.9% population of Earth – SLAVES – and almost the whole land – What if we made THEM ALL.. starting with Angelina Jolie.. Well excuse me this little "conspirationist" ;) digression. :P

BTW: DO you know that just ONE Rothschild owns the Bank of England [taken over hostile by another one back in XIX century] AND this very Bank of England practically owns FED so this ONE single Rothschild controls FED from his Inner City of London HQ? Just O N E man.. or the Vatican's wealth and that pope carrying some 5kg golden crucifix.. why not this cross to the starving ones and a wooden one for him? Be it good wood – oak.. [I am not sure about that Rothschild and his BoA bank but it cannot be confirmed because such data are top secret but I saw the BoA confirmation that TWELVE Rothschilds were Department directors through the history – the question is: WHY so many of them were those directors? Huh?]

Now I wait IMPATIENTLY for what Jolie, Pitt, Deep, De Niro, Willis, Rihanna, Madonna, Beyonce, Katy Perry, Clooney, Norton, Pacino and so on will do... They WOULD maybe be examples to follow for the remaining few HUNDREDS MILLIONS of richest people.. lots of millionaires and really a lot of multimillionaires.. [PLUS a few thousands of billionaires – including those who are NOT on the Forbes Top List for some reasons – maybe Forbes requires their consent and many do not give it – IDK]. I am speechless about these people.. however, I assume that the stars – the public icons should spend the most of their money on REAL, valid issues [not like deciding which NEXT CASTLE or JET to buy..] and THEN the world cabal maybe would in short time follow such examples.. maybe.. if not them then some rich people for sure..The Present situation is EVIL.

Winfrey is said to have donated the most of all stars on charity [$41Million] BUT she did not give money for the food for the hungry but for those in need for education access and programs for women and children. Besides, she is net worth $2.9Bil.. what she has donated is ONLY 1.5% of her total wealth.. drop in the sea.. and she is called a PHILANTHROPIST [sic!].. read more here:

http://www.aceshowbiz.com/news/view/00037338.html

In the meantime I charge you all '"TOP CLASS"' people GUILTY of failure to help – CRIME OF NEGLIGENCE! YOU ARE EVIL! Until you PAY! A LOT! Another issue is the "Elite" who govern the present socially-economically-politically-spiritually-religious [The] System so comfortable for them and who control human minds and hearts via the environmental programming. How to get to them? L8r. Now 1st things 1st. The rich must share. Period.

Get up, stand up, Stand up for your rights. Get up, stand up, Don't give up the fight. - Bob Marley

Don't gain the world and lose your soul, wisdom is better than silver or gold. - Bob Marley

4. The Gross World Product vs real incomes of the vast majority of the poor and the unequal and inequitable distribution of the Global Wealth

The above is the OFFICIAL data.. I suspect that less than 0.1% richest control half of the Global Wealth of which the immensely best part is concealed before Humanity..

The gross world product [GWP] is the combined gross

national product of all the countries in the world. Because imports and exports balance exactly when considering the whole world, this also equals the total global gross domestic product [GDP]. In 2012, the GWP totaled approximately US$84.97 trillion in terms of purchasing power parity [PPP], and around US$71.83 trillion in nominal terms. The per capita PPP GWP was approximately US$12,400.

Gross domestic product [GDP] dollar estimates are derived from purchasing power parity (PPP) calculations, per capita. Such calculations are prepared by various organizations, including the International Monetary Fund and the World Bank. As estimates and assumptions have to be made, the results produced by different organizations for the same country tend to differ, sometimes substantially. PPP figures are estimates rather than hard facts, and should be used with caution.

According to ILO [International Labor Organization] the World monthly average wage in Purchasing Power Parity dollars is $1'480. These dollars are not normal US dollars. The economists use specially adjusted exchange rates – one PPP dollar is equal to $1 spent in the US.

Essentially, the PPP dollar takes into account the fact that it is cheaper to live in some countries than others. The idea is that we don't care how many actual dollars somebody is paid in, say, China, but we care about what sort of stuff those dollars can buy.

"If someone in China takes their salary of 1,500 yuan per

month and they go to the bank, they will actually get $200 – ILO economist Patrick Belser explains – But this is not what we use to compute this global average, because what is important here is what people are able to buy with these 1,500 yuan, and this is where we compare to the purchasing power of the US dollars and find that it is actually equivalent to around $400."

"You might think that $1,480 a month, or $18,000 a year, is quite high. It comes to $75 a day for a 20-day working month – but it's well known that more than a third of the world's population lives on less than $2 a day. How can these two views of global incomes add up?"

Employment is no guarantee of escaping poverty, the International Labor Organization [ILO] estimates that as many as 40% of workers as poor, not earning enough to keep their families above the $2 a day poverty line. Source:

 http://www.bbc.com/news/magazine-17512040

The gross annual wages in given countries roughly equal their GDPs [PPP] per capita while the disposable annual wages vary from ca. 50% to even 100% depending on the compulsory deductions – like taxes. For instance in USA, Canada, Australia, Denmark, Switzerland and UK the average wage equals ca. 75% of the GDP [PPP] per capita; in Germany, Netherlands, Sweden, Norway, Austria, Italy, France and Belgium [some of the richest EU countries] +/-55%; in Spain, Greece, Israel and Finland ca. 62-65% and for example in Ireland and Poland almost 100%.

This all above shows that it is possible that the global average wage may almost equal the per capita PPP GWP. Let us assume the USA/UK/Australia variant of 75% PPP GDP – 75% of $12'400 is $9'300 and this would be the annual income for ALL of 3.1 billions employed people..

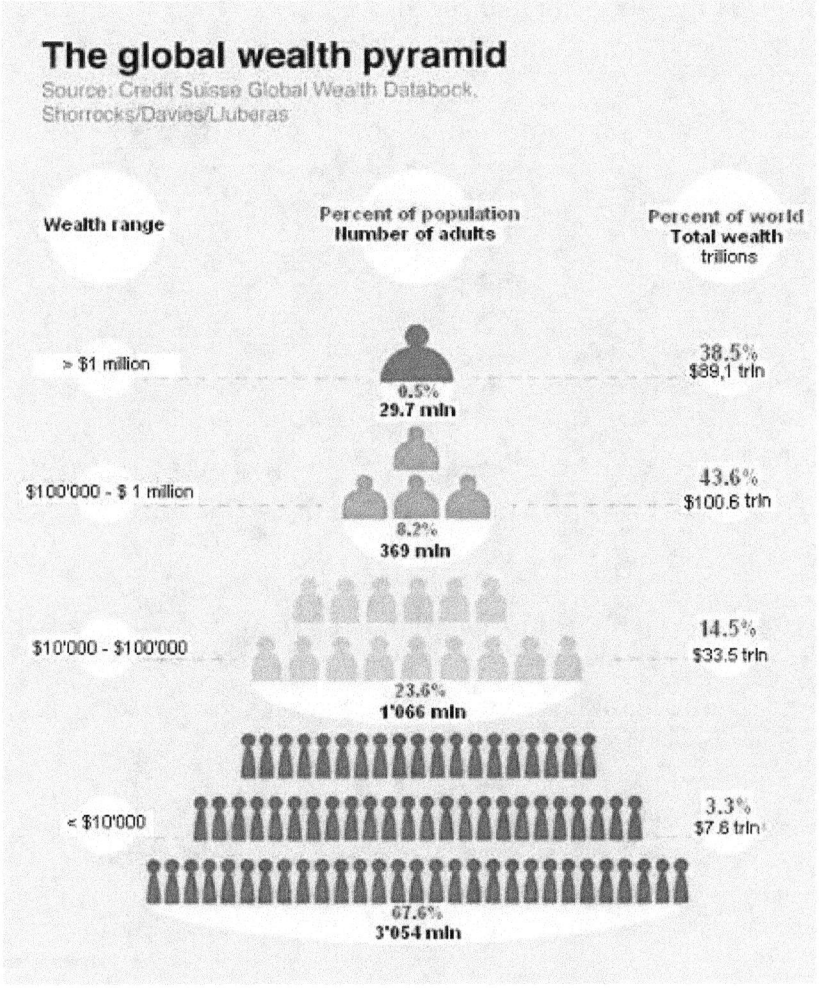

The global wealth pyramid

Source: Credit Suisse Global Wealth Databook.
Shorrocks/Davies/Lluberas

Wealth range	Percent of population Number of adults	Percent of world Total wealth trillions
> $1 million	0.5% 29.7 mln	38.5% $89.1 trln
$100'000 - $1 million	8.2% 369 mln	43.6% $100.6 trln
$10'000 - $100'000	23.6% 1'066 mln	14.5% $33.5 trln
< $10'000	67.6% 3'054 mln	3.3% $7.6 trln

The estimated World Labor Force is ca. 3'300'000 people and according to my data the world unemployment rate in 2012 was 6.1%. The world informal labor market is estimated at the volume of ca. $6.5Trillion which is ca. 8% of the GWP – seemingly rather insignificant – but it is

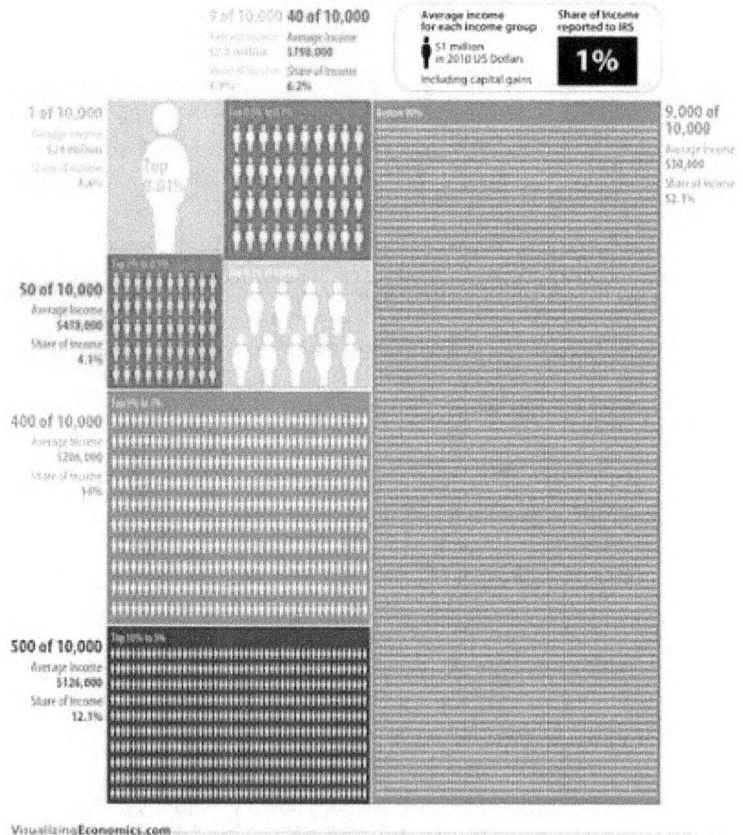

BLACK, INFORMAL market so how do they calculate it? Maybe it is $20Trillion [23% GWP] or $50Trillion [59% GWP] because of a few wealthiest men who make money on the black market for instance on diamonds, drugs, weapons and gold? Then the world monthly average wage as a function of GWP would be not $1'480 but almost $2'500!

Even if the official, formal average monthly wage is only $1'480 paid for each of 3.3Millions World Labor Force minus 6.1% unemployed = 3.1Bil employed people then we have to add the 8% [officially] informal labor market rate to $1'480 and this gives us $1'598 [official] real formal and informal average wage - $693 total per capita for ALL the people no matter if employed or not – and $2'772 per a standard family of four monthly - $33'264 annually]. This is really enough for living for the very vast majority of people. But IF the informal market labor market is very miscalculated and equals, say, modest $35Trillion [41% GWP] then we get the unofficial and informal but REAL average monthly wage $2'087 and respectively $921 a month = $11'060 annually per capita [all 7'150'000 human beings] and $3'684 monthly per each family of four - $44'240 annually. This would be the annual income for ALL the people – no matter if employed or not! Be it $33'264 annually per a family of four or $44'240 – I cannot say which one is more REAL – both figures mean this: This World can EASILY afford VERY decent living for EACH family on Earth.. for EVERY single person of 7'150'000'000 people IF the richest people defined the necessity properly, stopped their over-consuming way of life and SHARED their surplus with the poor..

61

This is the USA present income distribution system, what Americans think it is and what they chose to be ideal:

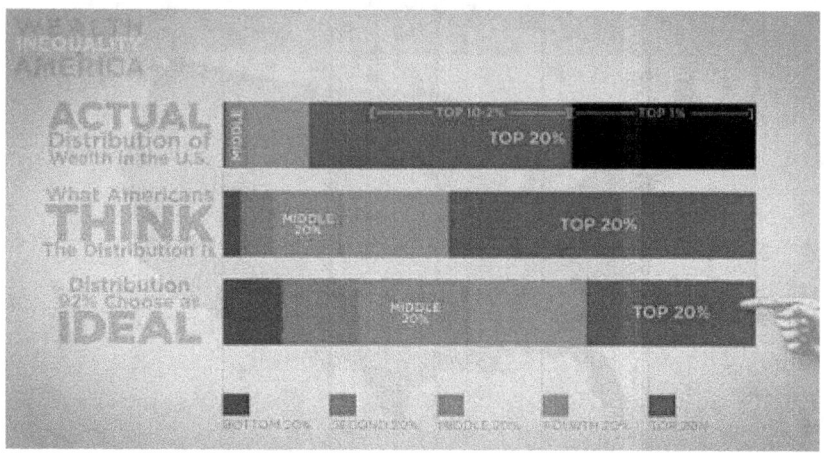

I am not saying that the EQUAL system would be FAIR and EQUITABLE.. Maybe the below system where the rich get some twice+ more than the poor is much better because it would provide better motivation for work.. still

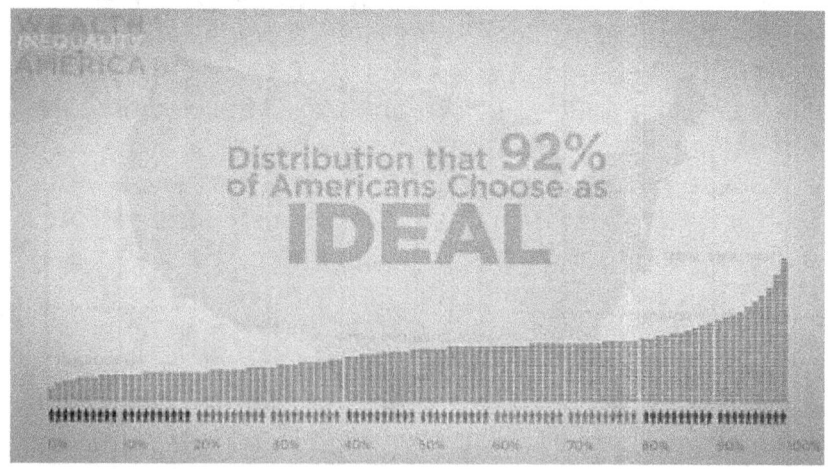

a WAY MORE equitable and fair than what we have nowadays.. But so far we have this:

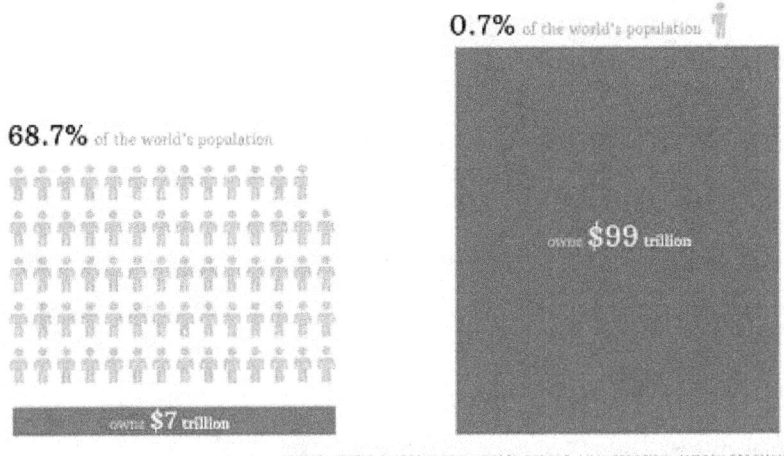

Another essential issue inseparably associated with income is wealth [money makes more money] The global Wealth by Credit Suisse is ca. $250Trillions and the top ca. 0.5% wealthiest people have ½ of that – OFFICIALLY. But I found out that some of the richest are not listed on Forbes World Billionaires List for one instance..

Digression: namely I found ONLY 2 Rothschilds on the list totaling at $3.2Billions and some other sources mention Evelyn Rothschild net worth $20Billions and Jacob Rothschild worth $5Billions – to conclude the whole Rothschild Dynasty is estimated roughly with $500Billions, though some sources say about $Trillions.

Therefore it is very likely that they are not counted by

Credit Suisse, either, as many other richest men – maybe even those who are in fact the RICHEST: a lot richer than Gates, Buffet or Putin – and the GW is for instance $314, $377 or $444 Trillions or a few Quadrillions, not $250Tril. If divided equally $250Trillions/7.15Billions people = $35'000 per capita – be it a child, adult or an elderly person [$140'000 per a family of 4]. If it is $444Trillions then we get $62'097 per capita [$251'848 per a family of 4] for all people on Earth.

True, real incomes and wealth are concealed by the rich and wealthiest for a whole variety of reasons: for instance to veil some of their gargantuan fortunes in order to avoid social unrests – the richest often keep their wealth in secrecy to avoid asking or begging for money, anger or robbing – this may happen either on small, individual scale or on a huge scale like country or global uprising or

rEvolution. It is entirely obvious that numerous richest LIE about their money because they are afraid that some day people who were under-payed [robbed] by them in major ways will stand up for what really should be theirs. And take it.

"To answer the failure of the capitalist system, the working class must advance a comprehensive, global socialist program, making a direct revolutionary assault on the fundamental causes of the crisis: private ownership of the means of production, and the division of the world into antagonistic nation-states, each dominated by a capitalist elite seeking to maximize its own profits and power. The working class must take the wealth of society, produced by its labor, into its own hands, by seizing the assets of the giant multinational corporations

Start where you are.. use what you have.. do what you can.. ~ Arthur Ashe

A year from now you may wish that you had started today.. ~ Karen Lamb and placing them in public ownership and under democratic control. The development of the world economy must then proceed on the basis of an international plan, drawn up to produce both rapid economic growth and the abolition of poverty and social misery, raising the living standards of working people all over the world to a decent level.

This program is neither Utopian nor far-fetched. On the contrary, it is the perspective of continued capitalist depression, social polarization and imperialist war that is unrealistic, even preposterous, from the standpoint of the interests of the vast majority of the human race."

https://www.wsws.org/en/articles/2012/05/pers-m01.html

Amazing facts about the richest man ever:

A very intriguing and interesting case is John D. Rockefeller believed to be the wealthiest in the history of mankind, according to Forbes 2008 List of Wealthiest historical figures. Rockefeller passed away in 1937 and was worth $1.4 billions - the equivalent of between US$392 to US $663.4 BILLIONS in today's dollar value - 2014 dollars - [in the thirties of XX one could buy a brand new car for ca. $1000 and ALL cars were considered LUXURY] He was the first American to ever be worth over $1 billion and donated over $500 million to charity upon his death. A list of Mr. Rockefeller's organized charities shows that he was chiefly interested in education and scientific medical research [ca. Half of his donations], the Baptist Church and other religious or social organizations. But $250 millions went to his own Rockefeller Foundation. He never gave a dime for food for the hungry!

As for his wealth:

He is estimated to be worth averagely $500 billions and ca. 1/3 of it went for charity as stated above but I have no clue what algorithm was used to count that.. The relevant online calculators mostly give the value of a 1937 $1 worth ca. 2014 $15 [inflation adjustment] . I will use this 15x factor further to count the REAL Rockefeller's wealth left today.

But before I count it my way I will simply take his 1937 $900 millions [$1.4 billions total wealth minus $500 millions donations upon death] and add the 77 years most probable profit to that.

Now let's have a look into Forbes World's Billionaires List: and what? ONLY 1 humble David Rockefeller Sr with humble $2.9Bil.. WTF?? He is the John D.'s grandson in chief of the whole wealth! Where did the 2014 $333 billions go [2/3 of 1937 $1.4 billions after $500 millions went on charity]??

SURELY Rockefellers DID made PROFIT on the 2014 $333 BILLIONS since 1937! OBVIOUSLY John R's fortune has been MULTIPLIED through 77 years! MONEY MAKES MONEY! And such money moguls very often make even 50% annually on their capital.. or even more.. But let's assume they were not as smart and made MODEST 7% average profit annually on it for 77 years.. I'll count this for you: 7% a year based on ca. $900 1937 year millions for 77 years [multiplied by the inflation adjustment factor - 15] totals:

ATTENTION!

{1.07x1.07x ... x1.07} 77 times ==> 183 times more:

$900'000'000x183=$164.7 BILLIONS
$164.7 BILLIONSx15=$2.47 TRILLIONS

BUT what if they were just a little bit smarter and made averagely 10% profit annually on $900 millions? Here you go: in 77 years they have 1539 times MORE:

$900'000'000x1539=$1.385 TRILLIONS

$1.38 TRILLIONSx15=$20.776 TRILLIONS

..1/10 the OFFICIAL Global Wealth.. owned by 1 family..

BUT IF they were just a little bit smarter and have made 15% a year we are getting to astronomical:

$900'000'000x47'177=$42.46 TRILLIONS

$42.46 TRILLIONSx15= $637 TRILLIONS

And if they made, say. 20% annually on their capital, then even without the 15 inflation factor today they'd have:

1250132x$900'000'000=$1.13 QUADRILLIONS

Impossible?

So I ask you again Rockefellers: **WHERE DID THE MONEY GO?**

And I answer [Ockham's Razor]:

You CONCEAL your wealth.. THEN WHY???

..to avoid social unrest.. uprisings.. rEvolution..

Many people believe that for instance Rothschild Dynasty control over $1 trillion in real estate and banking assets alone. Their net worth alone is estimated at well over $100 trillion by some people.. others talk about $500 Trillions..

http://topinfopost.com/2014/02/11/the-master-of-the-world-rothschild-banking-dynasty

The list of the richest men in the history mentions John D. Rockefeller, Carnegie, Vanderbilt, Mellon, Henry Ford, Marcus Crassus - all are estimated in HUNDREDS OF BILLIONS and dead way before the World war II and to all of their families we may use the reasoning and calculations adequate to that which I used to discern the John D. Rockefeller's wealth.. Does that mean that the official data on GWP and GW is but a horrendous hoax aimed to maintain the System calm and quiet?? And do thus the few richest family dynasties most probably control the total Global Wealth?

http://www.neatorama.com/2008/07/09/10-richest-people-of-all-time-and-how-they-made-their-fortunes/#!bOGM3k

My conclusion is that the official Global Wealth seems to be utterly different from the True, REAL GW which is kept in secrecy to evade imminent social unrests and/or uprisings if the people realized that GW and Global Income come not in several trillions but most probably quadrillions.. **Let's assume humbly that the real GW is some 10x bigger - $3Quadrillion and adequately the Global Income [officially 1/3 of GW] is $1Quad..** THEN the annual Global Income per capita would reach $140'000 [$560'000 per a standard family of four] and the Global Wealth shared equally among all people would be $420'000 per capita **[1.68Mil per a standard family of 4]**

5. My thoughts on the present sick and inequitable socially-economically-political world system and the need for Lightning Evolution of Humanity: rEvolution

I wanna share a few thoughts on the rEvolution [I would say Lightning Evolution] with you. Questions like: Goals, ideas. Why revolution? How? What to do? The Dark Shadow Elite: Who are they? What do they do? What they don't. What we don't. Connections. What are they? What should be done? What is being done? What's not? Solutions, etc..

What I believe in is that SOMETIMES if necessary.. if no other way we DO need to fight for Freedom, Equity, Love, Truth and our LIVES. LITERALLY. PHYSICALLY. I rather avoid physical conflict and violence for almost all cost but NOT in the clear and present danger to the lives of my precious ones, myself included. For instance. AND lives are sometimes endangered because of the threat to exactly Freedom, Equity, Love or Truth.

I say rather Lightning Evolution or rEvolution than Revolution so the rich and cowards do not panic ;) lol! :D This is not any complete and final plan for anything but just a sketch, concerning only chosen matters [though I do hope that some of them are most vital] draft to be revised, discussed, changed, enriched, some things maybe should be removed BUT I guess that this work touches the core of the problem to be solved..

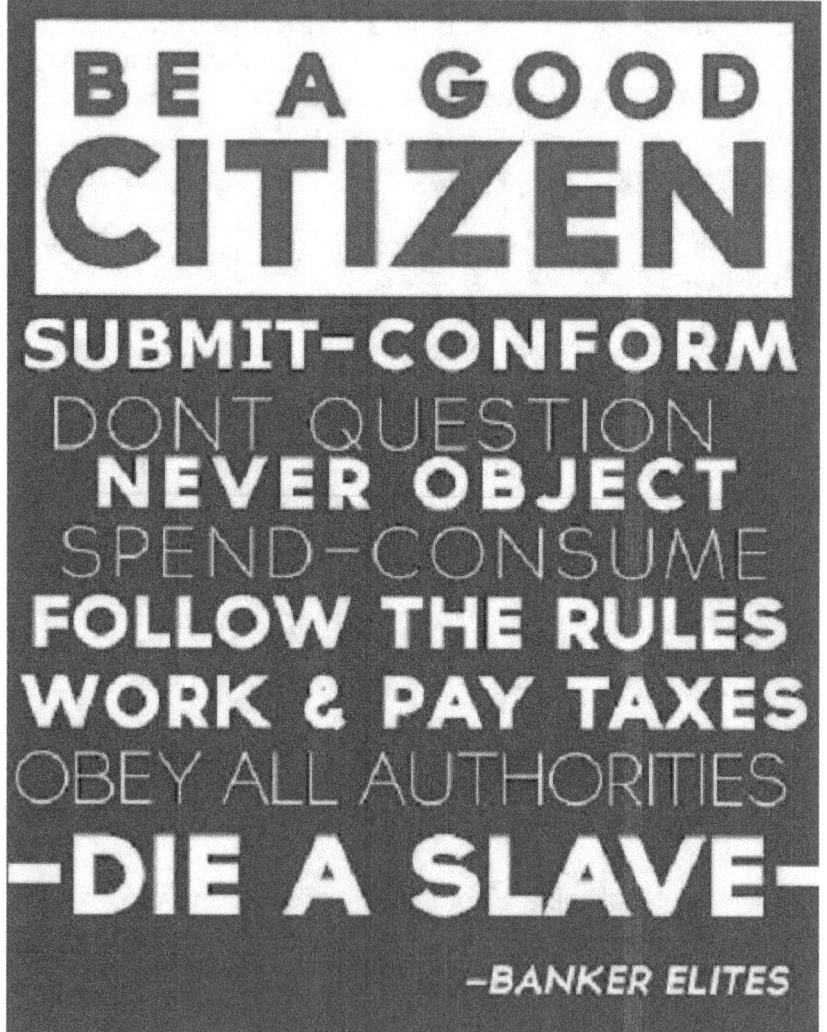

As long as enough people can be frightened, then all people can be ruled. That is how it works in a democratic system and mass fear becomes the ticket to destroy rights across the board.

James Bovard

First of all IN MY HUMBLE OPINION the global ascension - rEvolution of Humanity will take place NOT DIRECTLY through the sophisticated studies and theories of the awakened OR self-style awakened ones like Icke, Haramein, Braden, Kavassilas or Alex Jones OR Mayans, Atlantis, Ashtar Command, Ascended Masters, Anunnaki, Nibiru, Supernovas, Black Holes, Aliens, Huna, Shamans, Magic, Fairies, religion, group meditation, Dragons, Gods, Angels and Elves or whatever else fits this set. Hopefully you are able to see the connection here. But SOME of those may be helpful.

And the myth that some 144'000 are needed to start this off is bullshitte. What is needed is 7'150'000'000. All of us. We are all in this together. I state that this CAN be done rapidly in a Lightning Way IF the potentially strongest of us help the others instead of.. you know what.. they do not give a shit on the most..

Possibly the biggest obstacle is something so simple and known by most of you too very well.. FEAR. Fear is the antagonist of Love. Love=Live[Life] ERGO if you fear you are not alive in shortest words. There are some among us who do not fear, we untrained ourselves of it to a great degree. We have a duty to teach the others how to do it.

But we must also take down this most sick socially-economically-politically-spiritually-psychologically-philosophically-religious system of this whole planet which spoiled minds, hearts and souls.

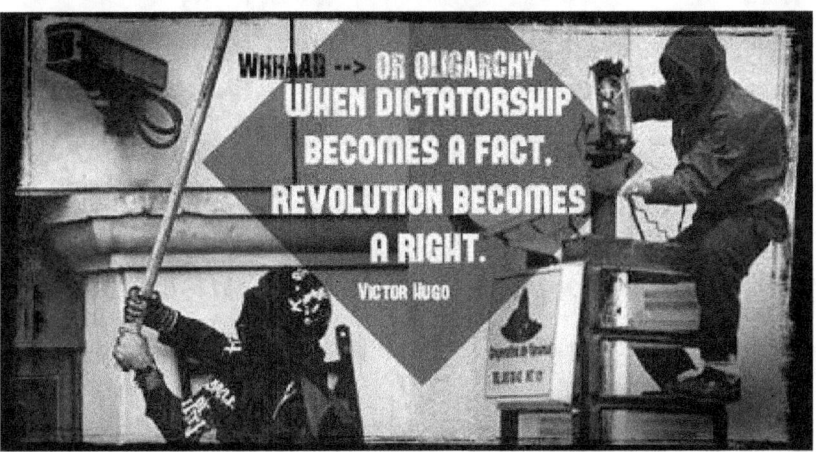

One happy day politics will hopefully be no more –
redundant – but before that happens, for now I see
the Socialistic Monarchy aimed at serious reducing
of the socially-economic gaps as the best system.
With elected king or queen – no royal bloodlines,

simply the best of all men – the strongest, the wisest, most loving and compassionate – the MLK-Gandhi-Solomon-King Arthur-Buddha-Gesar-Jesus type more or less to decide ultimately what is good for the whole planet and humanity in co-operation with his Elder's Council [not necessarily by their age] instead of endless, stupid and corrupted debates of mostly stupid and arrogant people over mostly irrelevant matters in the parliaments. And his Elder's Council would consist of the members of the same traits as his. The king I imagine should be elected by the former King's Elders' Council or maybe some other group of wise men, too. And a few King's Governors/Lords in a few regions of the world. And he is to serve – not RULE. That's all.

Epic of King Gesar [He was roughly an Eastern version of our King Arthur]:

 http://en.wikipedia.org/wiki/King_Gesar

Simplicity is the ultimate sophistication – Leonardo da Vinci

The present situation is so complicated, difficult and unknown in general to the people that there are much more questions than answers. Some dark, shadow forces seem to be very responsible and guilty and in the same time capable of turning the world into Paradise in an instant. For them it is a piece of cake. Or Hell – even easier – we are close – at least some 3 billions of human

78

beings are – not to mention all other Earthlings.

While numerous men try to find answers and solutions for ages, now that the situation became really dramatic at the break of the XX and XXI centuries still we have Nothing, I say. So I am researching lots of possibilities which 99,9% people reject, deny or disbelieve straight away and may ridicule myself as well. I mean UFO, crop-circles, demons, Archangels, Astral travels, dragons, gods and deities, aliens, Satan, God, Zeta, Vega, Arcturus, Pleiades, telepathy, clairvoyance, tarot, channeling, telekinesis, elements, history, economy, psychology, TV, Hollywood, SF literature – oh yes there must be more.

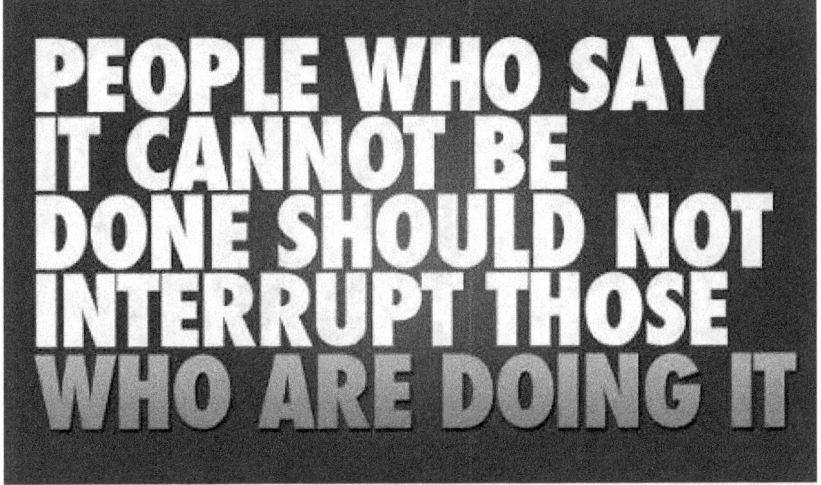

PEOPLE WHO SAY IT CANNOT BE DONE SHOULD NOT INTERRUPT THOSE WHO ARE DOING IT

Simply I don't reject anything a priori, I am open, I synthesize data from all areas as I can, talk to people with real experience and knowledge – I look for questions, answers and solutions and more. I consider the issue of the guilt for the state of the world and humanity is vital and crucial because a few bad kings and queens – the rulers and lords of Earth – have to be thrown under the bus. Really highest time. And I do hope and do imagine and believe that they can already see the wheels approaching really fast fast. The answers in this field may show who and what must go if anything should change for better. And they will bring more answers or proper questions.

[You may equally replace "afraid" with "shy" above.]

As the whole topic is very broad and elusive, history is a lie, men are fools, liars and cowards in general, level of deception and ignorance – unimaginable. Reliable and true data – rare and.. all dangerous – It is EXTREMELY difficult to create any satisfying, reliable, precise and concise Vademecum, source, guide-book, encyclopedia or book that would contain EVERYTHING IMPORTANT for this issue, for the rEvolution – Lightning Evolution – a guide-book which would ask all proper questions and give all true answers. A source which has it all and is TRUE and FULL – I bet you know what I mean here.

So for now what I write is more questions than answers and chaotic and maybe funny and sometimes wrong – but this is the way it is supposed to be right now. At this stage I primarily focus on my own and others' searches and delivering original, new and fresh ideas and data. Also I often cut off science or history or "reality" because they have not delivered the answers and solutions so far for 1000s years. So maybe the answers are beyond. And since nobody is willing to write such a wide analysis [though still limited] I take this responsibility. Gladly.

You are not a sheep

Stop acting like one

Time to throw the king under the bus.

[I.e. a few bad Kings and Queens]

To prove and evidence anything here – hard. For me it is not a question of debates, evidence and long wise discussions. You either do something or not. So far in the recent history people were MAINLY talking hours, weeks and decades, they also LOVE debates – well I don't. It is like telling the good from evil – you either do tell them or you don't. But you really cannot explain fully how you do that to the people who would like to be able to do that to. So you either on the bus or out of the bus [some under ;)] Here you go, I will be grateful for any comments and notes.

The ALMOST only reason that we have no war is that ALL MAIN WORLD POWERS have nuclear arsenals which are capable of destroying not just Earth but probably also Mercury, Venus and Mars or even the whole Solar System [it is enough to destabilize it critically for that to cause its imminent disintegration]!

The second main reason I see is this: No existing Coalition or Alliance can guarantee that the [present] Enemy is quickly, efficiently and entirely destroyed before any effective retaliation. If there was such an agreement – then we might have a 30 minutes of war here. Few billions of corpses. New free land, maybe a bit burnt and radiated. Less CO2. That's it. Clear. Eugenicists take over the world.

I have not slept for 30h. At about 3am I finished watching Boondock Saints II: ALL SAINTS DAY – quite good sequel to the cult 1999 Boondock Saints. I strongly recommend these 2 movies. Just watch them. Full movies available on youtube. :D And then a thought came to my mind: THE OIL IS ALREADY REDUNDANT, OBSOLETE. The shadow elite puppet masters [Bushobamas, Putins or Merkels] do not let the new technologies [there are cars running on clean water!] become the reality for at least one very good reason:

Let me put it in this way – Can you even imagine WHAT would happen in the Middle East area [most Arabic OIL POWERS] IF they faced the fact that their OIL IS ACTUALLY WORTHLESS? Most of these countries live ALMOST ONLY ON OIL! This is usually their major if not ONLY SIGNIFICANT INCOME! So there probably would be WAR then. I do not know if I am right here but please imagine that this hypothesis IS CORRECT. Just imagine – Would any of THEM [TPTB] tell us that we do not need oil or gas?

You should never wear your best trousers when you go out to fight for freedom and truth.

Henrik Ibsen

Saying "They" usually in such context I refer to the "evil shadow elite rulers of the world". The point here is that I do not know who they are. But maybe some do know it and have the according data, evidence and intel. Maybe the "enlightened" ones. ;)

Hypothesis:

No matter where the shit hits the fan – all roads lead to the inner City of London and Rohschild's Bank of England first of all as the World Bank in control of FED and IMF [and thus UN and Europe] and secondly to Vatican as spiritual power and authority and USA as simply English vassal, colony and barracks. And the same concerns Canada, New Zealand, Australia, India, the Republic of South Africa, Wales, Scotland and Ireland: my hypothesis is that de facto they are still English colonies, vassals as they used to be in the past in terms of huge influence of England with its queen who solely appoints the Lords in the House of Lords [in UK and Canada via her governor] which in fact may be much more powerful than people think and stronger than The House of Commons – but this is all veiled behind English propaganda and media dis-info curtain. IMHO. For them all that matters is gold. Mammon is the Arch-devil of GREED. GREED AND CORRUPTION OF THE TOP MONEY MAKERS is exactly what occupywallstreet was all about! And I really am not against the Israeli people or Jews at all. The same concerns Germans despite of their Hitler, Adolf or Russians with Trotsky and Stalin.

Conclusion: The whole planet is English Empire and the sick socially-economically-politically-spiritually-psychologically-religious SYSTEM in fact is English TYRRANY [and no wonder that English is the most popular language - like Latin in ancient Rome]

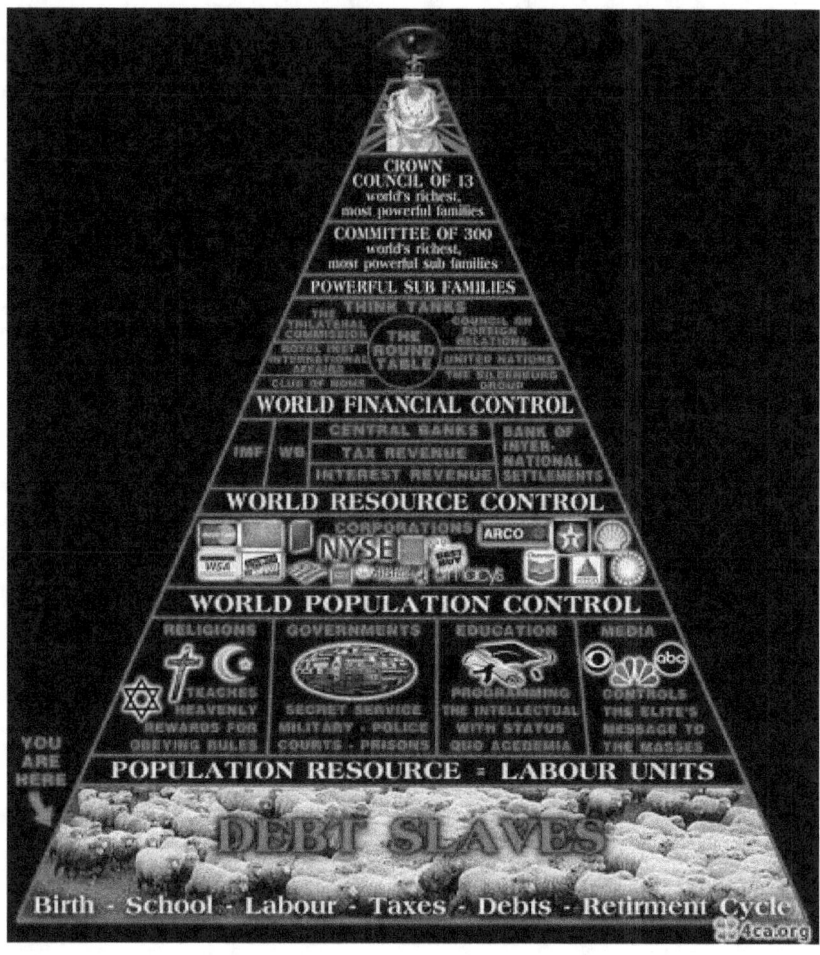

Of course one must not underestimate the gigantic role of media in sustaining The System.

THE MOST DANGEROUS WEAPON IS NOT A GUN...

THE MOST DANGEROUS WEAPON IS A GOVERNMENT CONTROLLED.

MEDIA!!

CAUTION:

The media is NOT a reflection of **reality.**

There's always[?] something specific about a given nation and ALL [all? Hmm..] nationalities have their scumbags, murderers, rapists and "evil shadow elite". Just some seem to give more [?] of this slime to the rest of the world. If I were to judge [and I am not] I would just pick the few worst of "Them" and nobody would see them any more [but I do not have the evidence who they are which is essential for the judgment]. I imagine this could really be an emergency solution for start. I also imagine that of course further plan is needed. But planning may concern some demo[crap]tion, vo[mi]ting or court trials for years or their justice owned by THEM and affected by THEIR media so it is too complicated for such a simple lonely guy like me. So I rather imagine that I would stay at the [so-called] lightning the torch for now or maybe I am pulling the trigger already..

Even in the USA 36.3 million people – including 13 million children – live in households that go hungry part of the time.

Those that master statistics, game theory, probability.. they are the ruling elite who owe you. The aim of the master is to make sure YOU CANNOT FORM a conviction. More than billion people go to bed hungry every day. $30Bil is enough to meet and deal with the World Hunger and sanitation [clean water!] for the whole year. I imagine that we could buy for example 10Bil kg=10Mil tones of some flour for $1/1kg. This would provide 10kg of flour annually to each of the hungriest men – 1 billion people – 10kg of flour per person a year IS A LOT! IT IS ENOUGH for them because they also have some their own supplies.

Furthermore I think that flour may be much cheaper on the wholesale of millions of tones. Most probably it is – so possibly that would be enough for even more, like 2 billions of men, to calm their hunger and save their lives. Of course it can be something better and cheaper than flour – maybe hemp seeds or some technology or jobs – WHATEVER! THIS CAN CAN CAN CAN CAN CAN CAN BE DONE! For these people it is not even a piece of cake. BUT SOME OF THEM WANT YOU DEAD AND DON'T MIND WATCH YOU DIE! DEFINITELY IT CAN SAVE THE 18'000 CHILDREN LIVES DAYLY. WITHIN THIS NUMBER CA. 5-8 THOUSANDS LITTLE BABIES!

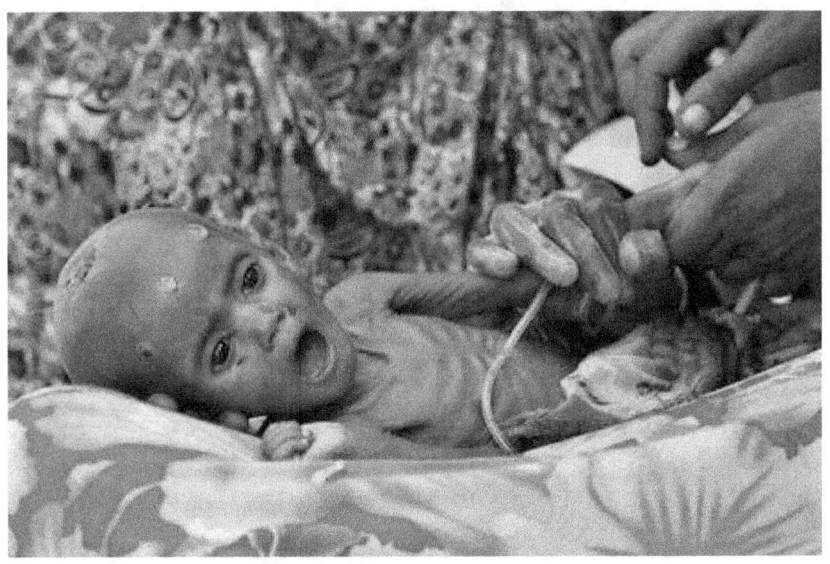

JUST COMPARE 30 BILLION US DOLLARS TO THE $2+ TRILLION OF THE TOP 100 RICH MEN AT WWW.FORBES.COM! Or to the aggregate wealth of $6.4Trillion of the 1650 world billionaires. Obviously Forbes delivers ONLY the official legal incomes and assets – NOT THE REAL WEALTH! A good guess is that many of them have more. So 100 men alone are easily capable of saving millions of people annually from the DEATH OF HUNGER and lack of CLEAN WATER! ARE THEY DOING THIS? Don't these facts and thoughts just speak for themselves? WHO ARE THESE PEOPLE?

William Gates, Oprah, Pitt, Rockefeller! DAMN YOUR TINY FOUNDATIONS! You better kill yourself and just leave the money to the poorest!

WAA-HOOO! THIS IS T E R R A!

$30 billion per year is needed to end world hunger.

$660 billion per year is the amount Congress spends on Defense.

Http://borgenproject.org/the-cost-to-end-world-hunger/

Do you know that the Global Wealth 2013 by Credit Suisse is more than $240 Trillion? And this is only the official evaluation – the Global Wealth is very difficult to measure especially that many wealthiest men would be willing to conceal their wealth as well as their income.

Did you know that 30 million richest men who have more than $1 million totally have officially {!!!] ca. 100-$150Trillion – 0.42% richest men have a half of world's wealth? 0.43% richest people have the total wealth equaling roughly the aggregate wealth of the remaining 99.38% PEOPLE! **IS THIS OK WITH YOU?**

It is said that the Rothschild Dynasty total wealth is $500Trillion. Do you believe that the total Rothschilds' wealth exceeds FOUR times the total wealth of those 30 million richest men AND that it exceeds TWICE the GLOBAL WEALTH? And how do you imagine ANYONE'S wealth exceed the GLOBAL wealth? OR does the Credit Suisse provides us with fake data? Dis-info? But who knows – maybe such fortunes like $100Trillion do exist. And maybe the Rothschild are such a case.

John Rockefeller is said to have been net worth ca. $664Billion in modern US dollars.. in 1937 when he died.. He was a "philanthropist" but he only donated ca. 1/3 of his fortune on medical research and education and never gave a dime to the 100s millions of the hungry people.. Just imagine how much may be the Rockefeller Dynasty's worth NOW.. I counted the probable variants for you in the previous chapter..

And there is ONLY 1 humble Rockefeller, David on Forbes List with $2.9Billion.. well.. that's just IMPOSSIBLE! This MUST be a CON! And certainly there are MANY like Rockeffelers..

There are theories that Rothschild Dynasty wealth totals $500Trillion. I suspect that this might be a translation mistake [don't tell me it is IMPOSSIBLE 100%] but maybe not.

Assume
NOTHING

Question
EVERYTHING

OPEN Your Eyes

CHALLENGE
The Opposition

And Start
THINKING

European languages behave in 2 ways as far as the main numbers over 1 million are concerned:

I million, billion, trillion, quadrillion, etc..

II million, milliard, billion, trillion, etc..

1st group of languages have the same system as English numbers and the 2nd has 1 more main number between million and billion – it is Milliarde, miliard, milliardo, etc... equal to English billion.

1. When you translate "billion" from English into the below languages you get "billion" as well: Spanish – billon; Latin – billion; Portugese – bilhao; Maltese – biljun; etc..

2. On the other hand, if you translate "billion" from English into Polish, German or Italian you get Milliarde, miliard, miliardo, etc...

Now imagine that the $500Trillions Rothschilds' wealth is in fact $500 billion and was just wrongly translated – firstly from English to German as "billion" [not "Milliarde" as it should be] and then the other way round into English as "Trillion" – I guess this is the case here, but am not sure.. I guess they have MANY Trillions..

Obviously such SHOCKING wealth of the Rothschild was likely to be widely published. What a discovery! But maybe the Rothschild like it because it proves their endless power .. or maybe they have another agenda.. or maybe I am wrong..

Obviously even modest $500Bil is a lot of money and would buy them some 10+ least developed countries and put them of the top of Forbes' with 10x more than Gates has AND most definitely would allow them to control the whole world economically to a great degree [unless there are even bigger fortunes but NOT listed by Forbes NOR taken into account by the Credit Suisse – WHICH I actually VERY strongly suspect even if only for the example of ONLY TWO humble Rothschild in the Forbes' billionaires list with the total of $3.2Bil.. where is the rest of the Dynasty?

/I found for instance Evelyn Rothschild net worth of ca. $20Bil in another source/

http://www.forbes.com/billionaires/list/#tab:overall_search:Rothschild

In the same way more richest people may conceal their fortunes and income – obviously a good guess is that many do that] And that Global Wealth estimated by the Credit Suisse instead of $240Trillion in such case [deliberate dis-info] might be as well even $2.3Quad or $23Quadrillion. And the REAL Global Wealth volume is top secret because the REAL data could effect in uprisings or revolution maybe. For instance. Imho.

Never assume the obvious is true. - William Saffire

Assume nothing, question everything – James Patterson

Question everything. - Albert Einstein

Wisdom begins in wonder. - Socrates

*Truth is available only to those who have the courage to question whatever they have been taught.
- Deep Alignment*

Never assume the obvious is true. - William Saffire

Assume nothing, question everything – James Patterson

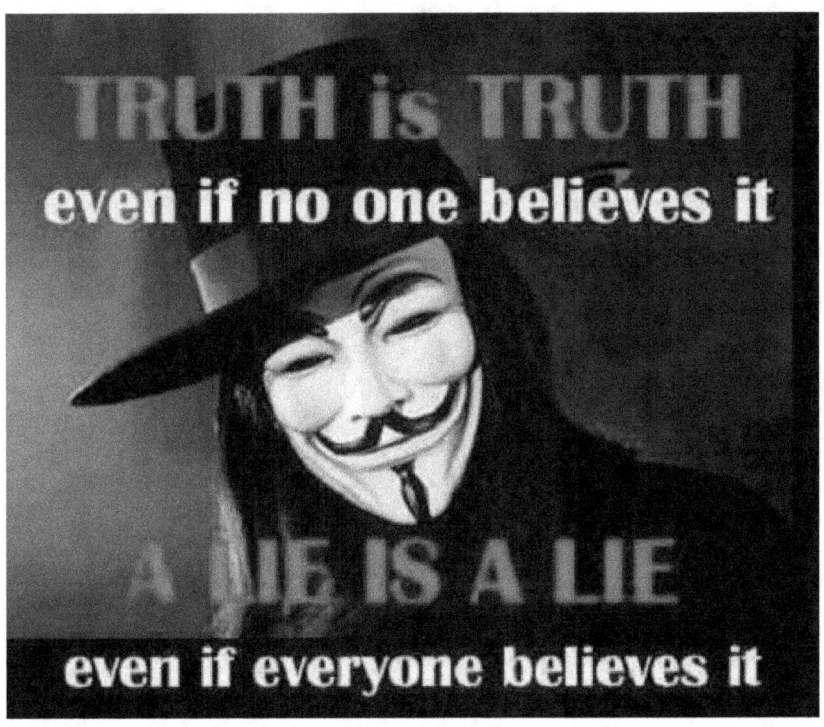

The cure for ignorance is to question. - Prophet Muhammad

Take the attitude of a student – never be too big to ask questions, never know too much to learn something new. - Og Mandingo

Once you stop learning you start dying. - Einstein

The important thing is not to stop questioning. - Albert Einstein

The hidden, shadow ELITE oligarchy – the True, Real Rulers of this World and 7Bil+ of their slaves.. Some of these Lords of the World are thought to be known like Rothschild, Morgan, Hapsburg, Buffets, Gates, Rockefeller, Vanderbilt, Mellon or Warburg OR the ENGLISH [not BRITISH] Queen but it is a good guess that quite a few do NOT want to be known and are NOT.. they rule the Earth from behind the curtains. Seemingly this world is on the most in the state of Peace but the socially-economically-politically-spiritually-psychologically-religious WAR between them – the Powers That Be and the humanity is just veiled, hidden and secret..

Hypothesis:

CEOs are earning $100'000s and millions and in the meantime 1.4Bil people are starving.. 2.8Bil live for less than $2 daily.. every 5s a child dies from hunger.. ca.6+ billions of people actually live in poverty [depended on the definition]..

Why is there minimum and NO maximum salary? This would solve the above problems and provide support for ALL poor people globally.. Solution: unite and fight peacefully for EQUITY because THEY are too proud and greedy to give it up without fight! Because THEY have career history, education and experience and thus DESERVE the zounds they are actually STEALING from the UNEQUAL, WORSE PEOPLE. We are the PEOPLE!

Don't say there's Nothing that THEY [the richest and the rulers of this planet] can DO about THE WORLD HUNGER. THEY can start with READING this book. EVERY 5s a child dies from HUNGER while some of THEM come on Facebook and say WE'RE ALL ONE and ALL IS ONE and therefore there is their New Agy concept of NO RIGHT NOR WRONG – No Good nor Evil and thus they program people into indifference towards Wrong, Evil.. mass callousness and also THEY do NOTHING about them [the children] because "that's what their souls need, their karma, their training grounds, kindergarten" and other BULSHITTE! AND has EVER the idea come into THEIR brains that it might be quite the opposite? That it's THEM under training in this KINDEGARDEN of THEIRS where THEY feel great like GURUS and they will ONLY be PROMOTED IF THEY HELP THESE CHILDREN AND THE PEOPLE?

FOR EVERY POSITIVE CHANGE YOU MAKE IN YOUR LIFE, SOMETHING ELSE ALSO CHANGES FOR THE BETTER - IT CREATES A CHAIN REACTION

[LEON BROWN]

Children are my main concern – ESPECIALLY these who live in Extreme Poverty like almost 3 billions people.. Almost half of the human population. $30Bil annually is enough to solve the global hunger problem but those who have the money do NOT share – instead we, poor ourselves would share with the poorer.

If you bother to count only the Forbes' Top 100 billionaires you will total $2Trillion+ that equal of world's 1/3 human population total annual income or the Domestic Product of ca. 50 least developed countries.. maybe more.. and realize that some of the richest may not want to be mentioned in Forbes and forbid it. Just the top 100 Forbes people practically OWN this planet and beyond it. This is because they FULLY CONTROL ALL EXISTING ASSETS. I did not even start to consider the Forbes Top 1650 billionaires – only the top 100! And we can only base on THEIR OFFICIALLY DECLARED WEALTH. Royalties and people who are rich because of their political position are not taken into account in the Forbes' Top Billionaires list.. How many such people are there, though? Well, one of them is Vladimir Putin with his net worth of $70Billions [officially ;)] which puts him on the 2nd position there right after Bill Gates.

It is beyond my imagination how these people can be affording luxuries in the face of just few such facts! How can they wear their diamonds? THEY ARE INHUMAN! LET THEM KNOW IT! And we are their SLAVES!

I state that taking down the present so very sick and severely inequitable socially-economical system – TYRRANY dominating on this whole planet is essential to free the people.. from FEAR [for instance about the

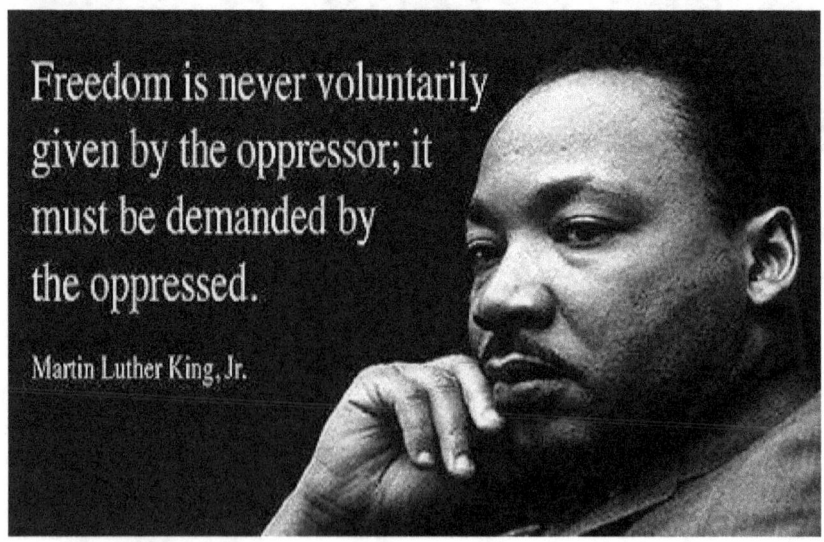

Freedom is never voluntarily given by the oppressor; it must be demanded by the oppressed.

Martin Luther King, Jr.

future] I state that this CAN be done rapidly in a Lightning Way IF the strongest of us help the others instead only standing up for themselves..

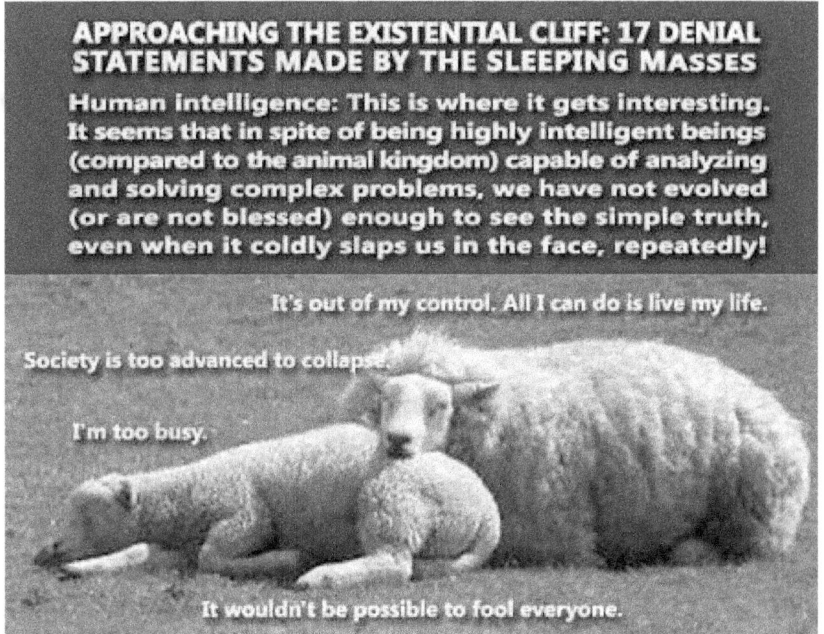

APPROACHING THE EXISTENTIAL CLIFF: 17 DENIAL STATEMENTS MADE BY THE SLEEPING MASSES

Human intelligence: This is where it gets interesting. It seems that in spite of being highly intelligent beings (compared to the animal kingdom) capable of analyzing and solving complex problems, we have not evolved (or are not blessed) enough to see the simple truth, even when it coldly slaps us in the face, repeatedly!

It's out of my control. All I can do is live my life.

Society is too advanced to collapse.

I'm too busy.

It wouldn't be possible to fool everyone.

Furthermore I state that the global awakening and ascension of humanity on many levels [not only spiritual but also social or economical] are essentially inhibited by one simple factor that probably we all are very familiar with, namely: FEAR which only few mention in their analysis of the relevant problems and solutions. I mentioned this issue earlier as possibly the biggest obstacle. Fear is the antagonist of Love. Love=Live[Life] ERGO if you fear you are not [fully!] alive in shortest words. It is associated closely with anxiety, conformity and cowardice. True Love cannot exist without Courage and therefore True Life cannot exist without it, and

101

neither Wisdom. There are some among us who do not fear, we untrained ourselves of Fear to a great degree. We have a duty to teach the others how to make it. So first things first. That's all.

I state that this all IS possible in no-time compared to all these fake theories like we need 144'000 or Mayans Knowledge or another Ashtar Command, Venusians from Pleiades or Aliens, abundance of channelings and ascendent masters and false belief that watching 5h movies and reading many "revealing&awakening" books will help significantly in that. Bullshit. [generally]. This is almost all waste of time. Mostly fiction.

Those movies and theories on the most steal your precious time [=ENERGY=LIFE] which you can sacrifice to achieve a lot more righteous and precious purposes. Youtube movies are not the most reliable source of information. As well as Wikipedia for instance. Besides

THEY, the Enemy can also plant their false data on youtube.. as well as all over the internet.. Their half-lies – best kind of deception – like 90% truth and 10% very valid lies – so you have an impression that it is truth but the 10% lies may totally damage the information as a whole as truth. No. We can help each other cause some of us are already a way beyond fear and can teach others how-to. And hopefully will. We are all in this TOGETHER. And in THIS notion we are all ONE. Because this is our CONNECTION.

"Without justice, there can be no peace. He who passively accepts evil is as much involved in it as he who helps to perpetrate it."

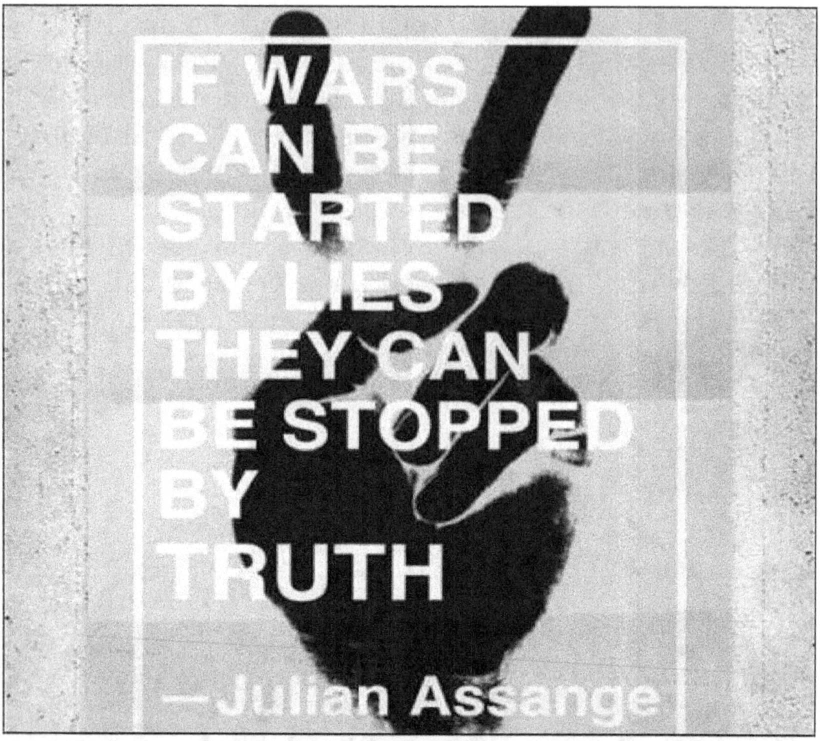

IF WARS
CAN BE
STARTED
BY LIES
THEY CAN
BE STOPPED
BY
TRUTH

—Julian Assange

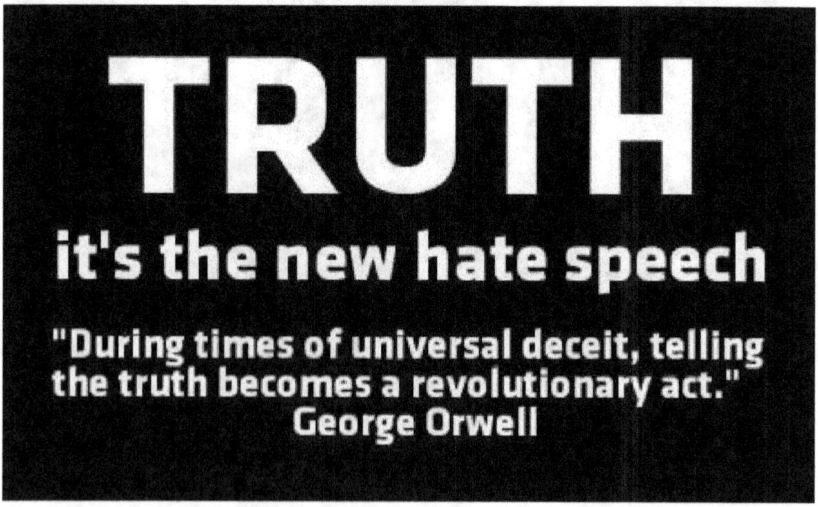

TRUTH

it's the new hate speech

"During times of universal deceit, telling
the truth becomes a revolutionary act."
George Orwell

WHAT DID I DO?

ABSOLUTELY, NOTHING.

Intelligence
without wisdom
brings
destruction.

Erol Ozan

meetville.com

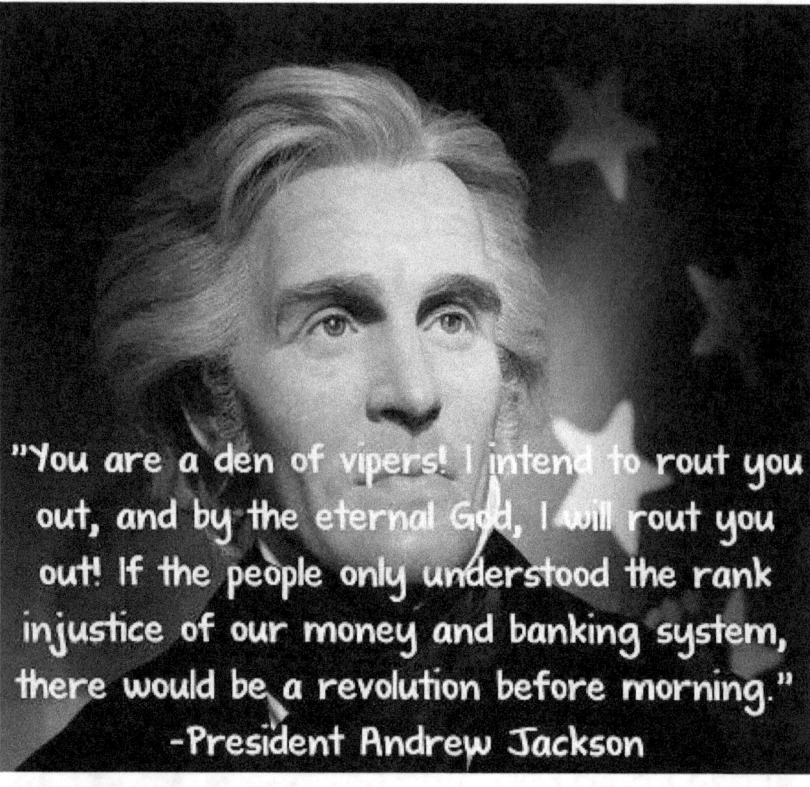

"You are a den of vipers! I intend to rout you out, and by the eternal God, I will rout you out! If the people only understood the rank injustice of our money and banking system, there would be a revolution before morning."
-President Andrew Jackson

"WHEN A WELL-PACKAGED WEB OF LIES HAS BEEN SOLD GRADUALLY TO THE MASSES OVER GENERATIONS, THE

TRUTH WILL SEEM UTTERLY PREPOSTEROUS AND ITS SPEAKER A RAVING LUNATIC."

~DRESDEN JAMES

"I will not let anyone walk through my mind with their dirty feet."
Gandhi

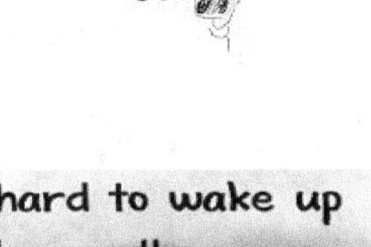

It's EXTREMELY hard to wake up those who only dream they are awake and/or pretend it. ~ Whhaad.

You can't wake a person who is pretending to be asleep.

Navajo Proverb

Once you wake up it's hard to go back to SHEEP. ~ Internet

"A lie doesn't become truth, wrong doesn't become right & evil doesn't become good, just because it's accepted by a majority."

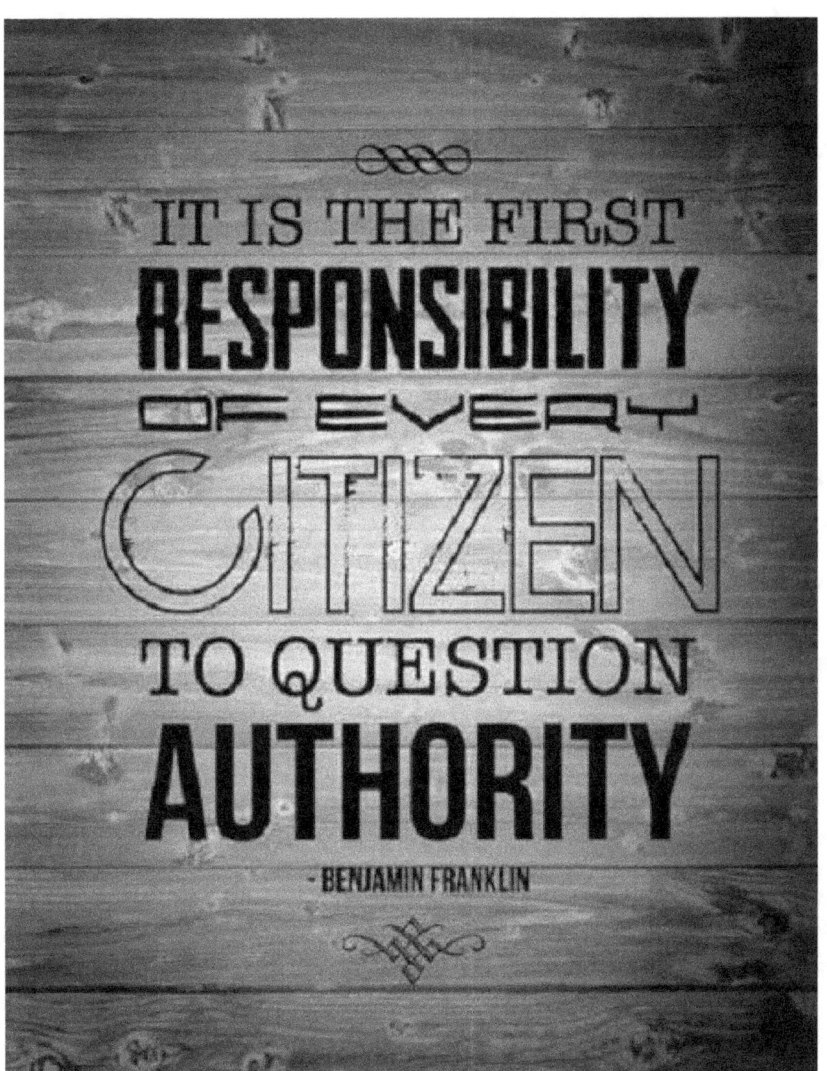

IT IS THE FIRST RESPONSIBILITY OF EVERY CITIZEN TO QUESTION AUTHORITY

- BENJAMIN FRANKLIN

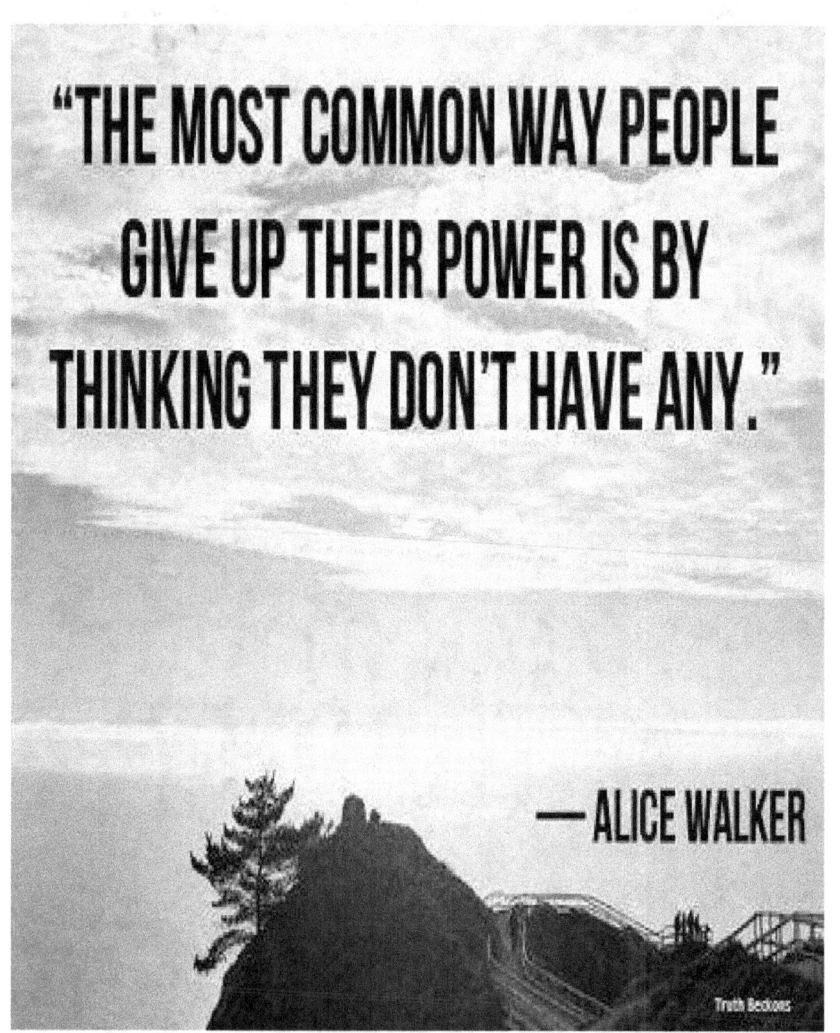

"THE MOST COMMON WAY PEOPLE GIVE UP THEIR POWER IS BY THINKING THEY DON'T HAVE ANY."

— ALICE WALKER

Truth Beckons

"THE GREATEST MISTAKE OF THE MOVEMENT HAS BEEN TRYING TO ORGANIZE A SLEEPING PEOPLE AROUND SPECIFIC GOALS. YOU HAVE TO WAKE THE PEOPLE UP FIRST, THEN YOU'LL GET ACTION."

-MALCOLM X

TOP Stars and the richest "HOUSES'".. or rather CHATEAUS:

Denzel Washington

next

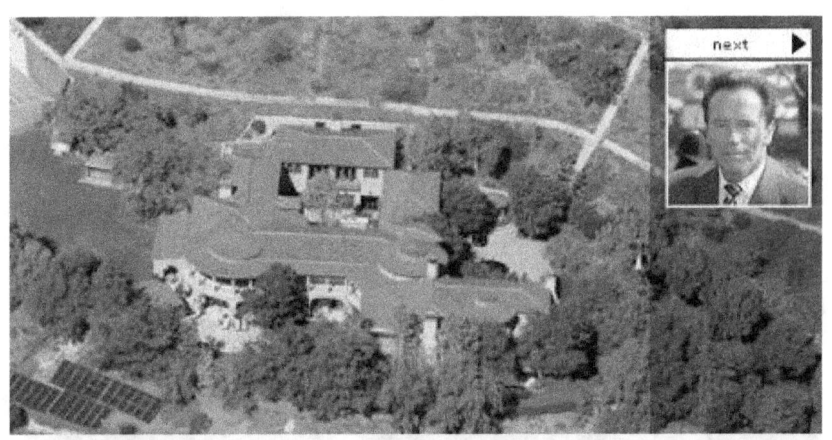

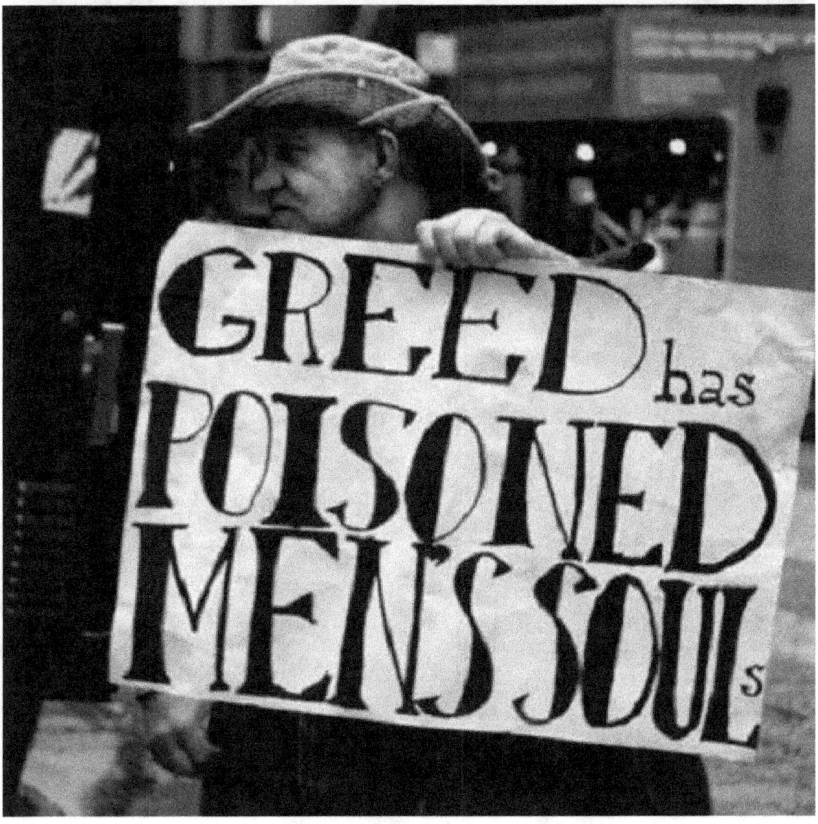
GREED has
POISONED
MEN'S SOULs

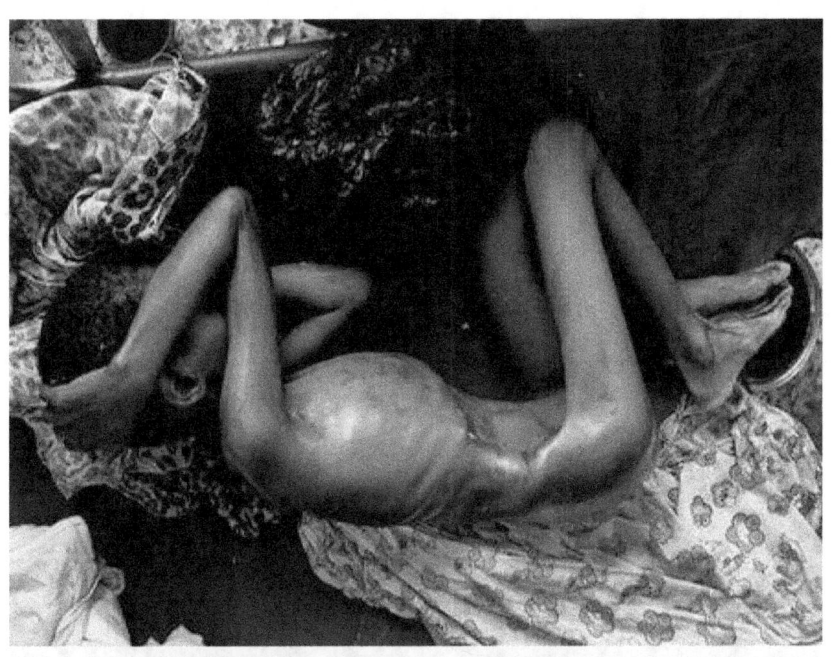

The world's hunger is getting ridiculous. There is more fruit in a rich man's shampoo than in a poor man's plate.

Habibies.com

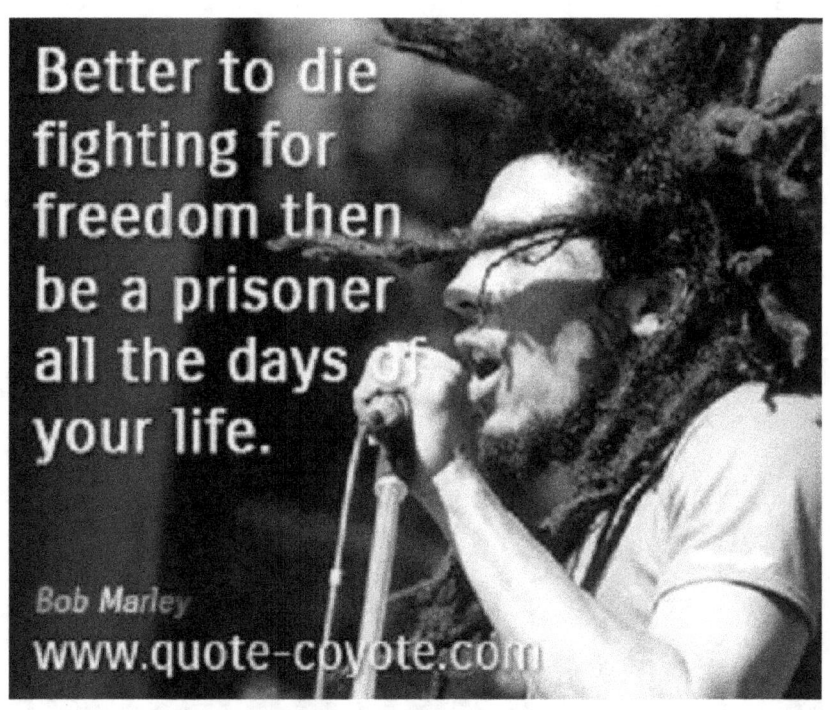

GREED has poisoned men' souls. ~ a man with a poster in the street (USA)

Don't gain the world and lose your soul, wisdom is better than silver or gold. - Bob Marley

Get up, stand up, Stand up for your rights. Get up, stand up, Don't give up the fight. ~ Bob Marley

Freedom deserves a fight and every fight deserves freedom!

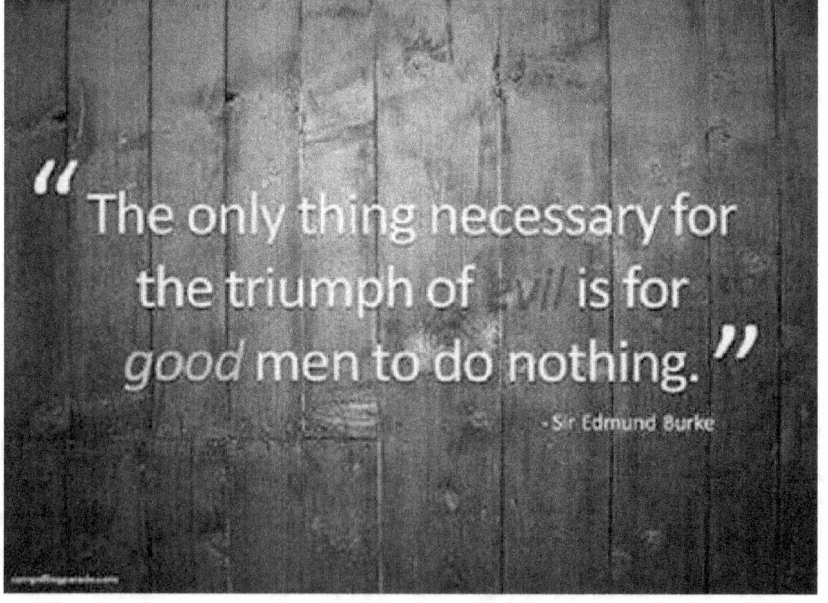

"The only thing necessary for the triumph of evil is for *good* men to do nothing."

- Sir Edmund Burke

He who passively accepts evil is as much involved in it as he who helps to perpetrate it. He who accepts evil without protesting against it is really cooperating with it.

Martin Luther King, Jr
American activist
(1929-1968)

QuoteHD.com

OUR LIVES BEGIN TO END THE DAY WE BECOME SILENT ABOUT THINGS THAT MATTER

Martin Luther King Jr.

celebquote.com

All tyranny needs to gain a foothold is for people of good conscience to remain silent.

—Thomas Jefferson

A MAN WHO
STANDS FOR
NOTHING
WILL FALL FOR
ANYTHING.

MALCOLM X

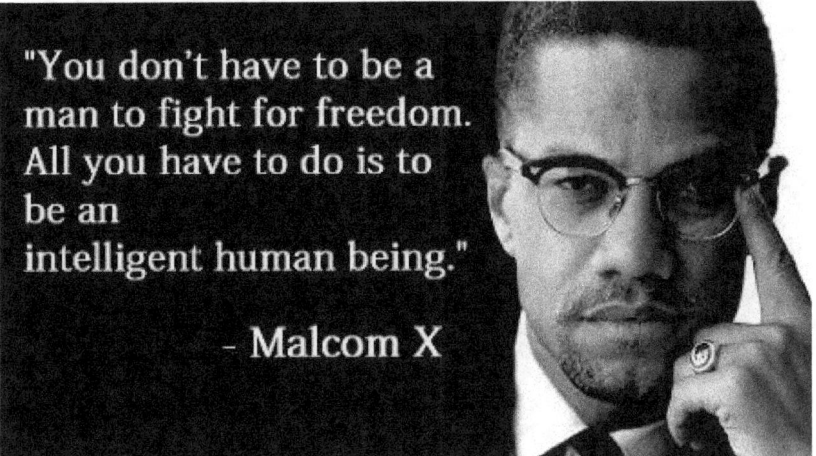

"You don't have to be a man to fight for freedom. All you have to do is to be an intelligent human being."

– Malcom X

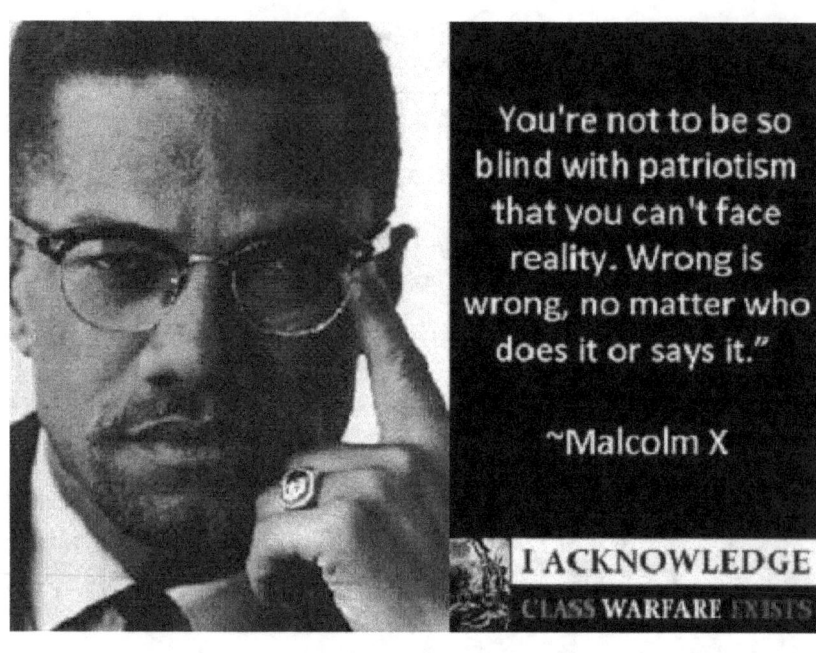

You're not to be so blind with patriotism that you can't face reality. Wrong is wrong, no matter who does it or says it."

~Malcolm X

I ACKNOWLEDGE CLASS WARFARE EXISTS

Our loyalties must transcend our race, our tribe, our class, and our nation; and this means we must develop a world perspective.

- Martin Luther King, Jr.

Created using www.PosterPin.com

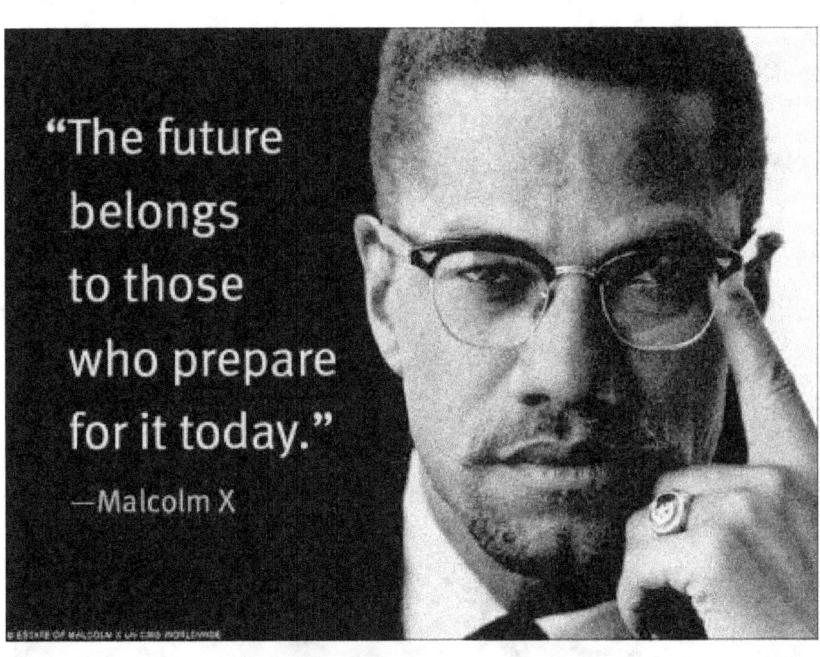

"The future belongs to those who prepare for it today."

—Malcolm X

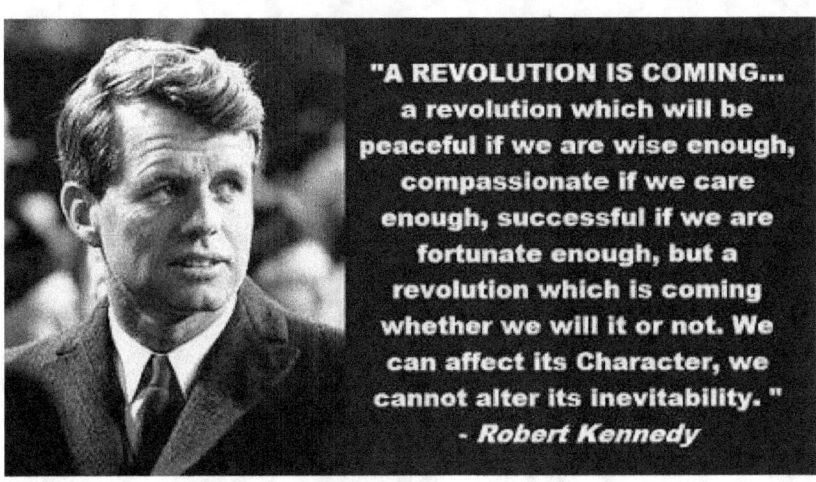

"A REVOLUTION IS COMING... a revolution which will be peaceful if we are wise enough, compassionate if we care enough, successful if we are fortunate enough, but a revolution which is coming whether we will it or not. We can affect its Character, we cannot alter its inevitability."
- Robert Kennedy

"There's a plot in this country to enslave every man, woman, and child. Before I leave this high and noble office, I intend to expose this plot."
~ Pres. JF Kennedy - 7 days before his assassination.

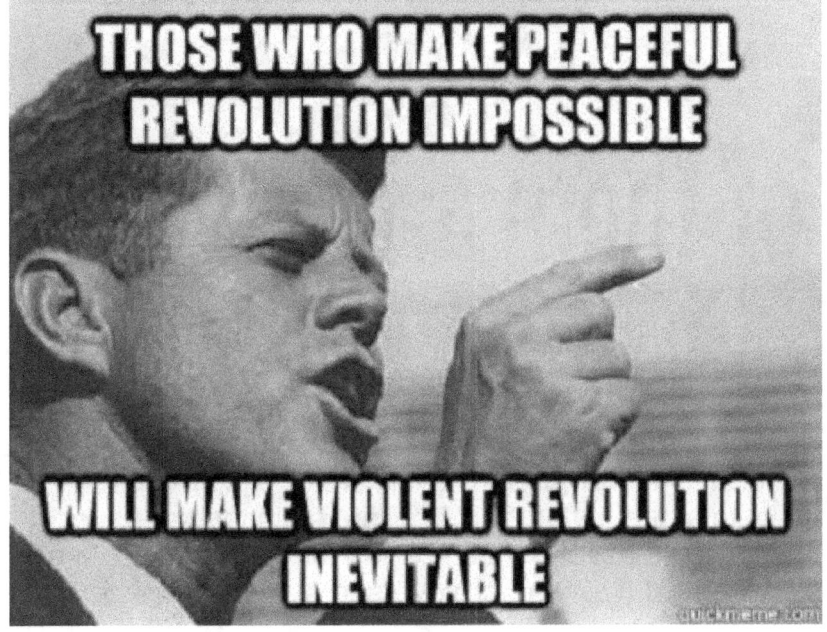

Some 1.4 billions people are starving on less than $1 daily

Every 3.6 seconds a person
dies of hunger

75%

# of them are children

Some 2.8 billions people live in EXTREME poverty on less than $2 daily

Some 6.5-7 billions people live in relative poverty performing under-payed slavery work [often over 10h daily] to make up for their families livelihood.. often to cover steered over-consumption and credits.. there are also those slaves who are overseers and taskmasters..

The Money required to eradicate hunger for everyone in the world has been estimated at 30 billion a year...about as much as the world spends on the military every eight days.

SLAVERY
It works better when you don't tell them.

"Nobody can give you freedom. Nobody can give you equality or justice or anything. If you're a man, you take it."

Malcolm X

It is said that some socially-economically-political systems proved wrong in the history.. It is said so about socialism, communism or monarchy or empire.. This is bullshitte.. those systems failed not so much because of their foundations but because of the stupid and thus Evil men who took over the power and governed them.. Each of these systems had some pros and if governed by the right, GOOD men could have proven right.. the most beneficial combination of the best foundations of these systems could provide an ideal system.. I confessed I am a socialist-monarchist.. I would add a pinch of communism and anarchy to that.. but then now they will call me "negative" names: anarchist, communist, socialist, monarchist.. because '"HISTORY TAUGHT US THAT THOSE WERE MISTAKES AND WE ARE WISER THAN THAT NOW AND WE DO NOT WANT TO REPEAT THEM"' but history is HISTORY! This is the PAST! What failed in the past can prove right in the FUTURE! Or NOW! In different circumstances.. different TIME.. with different people in power.. Besides, history is a LIE!!!

History on the most is written by the conquerors.. the winners.. those who are more greedy, violent, aggressive, deceptive, treacherous, cruel, insensible, sneaky, cunning >>> EVIL.

I recommend you to read the trilogy '"Lord of the Rings"' with King Aragorn and the cult '"Dune"' cycle by Frank Herbert with Emperors Paul Muad Dib and Leto II Atreides.. there are patterns of ideal monarchs in these books..

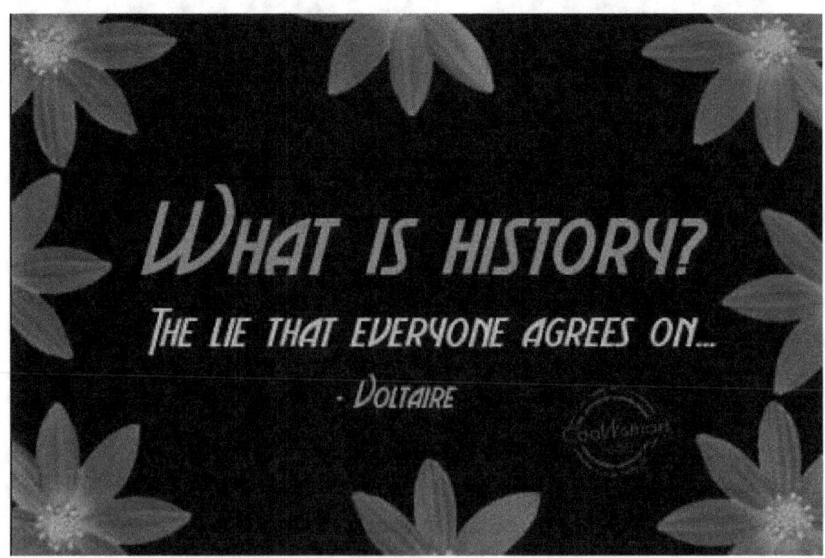

History is a set of lies agreed upon..

~ Napoleon Bonaparte

The history of our race, and each individual's experience, are sown thick with evidence that a truth is not hard to kill and that a lie told well is immortal.

(Mark Twain)

izquotes.com

"TRUTH IS SO OBSCURED NOWADAYS AND LIES SO WELL ESTABLISHED THAT UNLESS WE LOVE THE TRUTH WE SHALL NEVER RECOGNIZE IT."
-BLAISE PASCAL

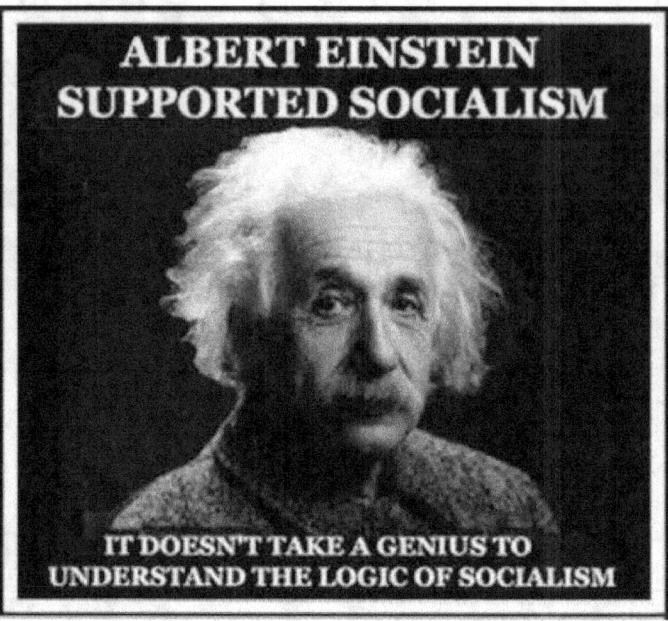

ALBERT EINSTEIN
SUPPORTED SOCIALISM

IT DOESN'T TAKE A GENIUS TO
UNDERSTAND THE LOGIC OF SOCIALISM

Albert Einstein
"Why Socialism"
Monthly Review, 1949

"There is no provision that all those able and willing to work will always be in a position to find employment; an 'army of unemployed,' almost always exists. The worker is constantly in fear of losing his job. Since unemployed and poorly paid workers do not provide a profitable market, the production of consumers goods is restricted, and great hardship is the consequence. Technological progress frequently results in more unemployment rather than in an easing of the burden of work for all. The profit motive, in conjunction with competition among capitalists, is responsible for an instability in the accumulation and utilization of capital which leads to increasingly severe depressions. Unlimited competition leads to a huge waste of labor, and to that crippling of the social consciousness of individuals..."

Albert Einstein

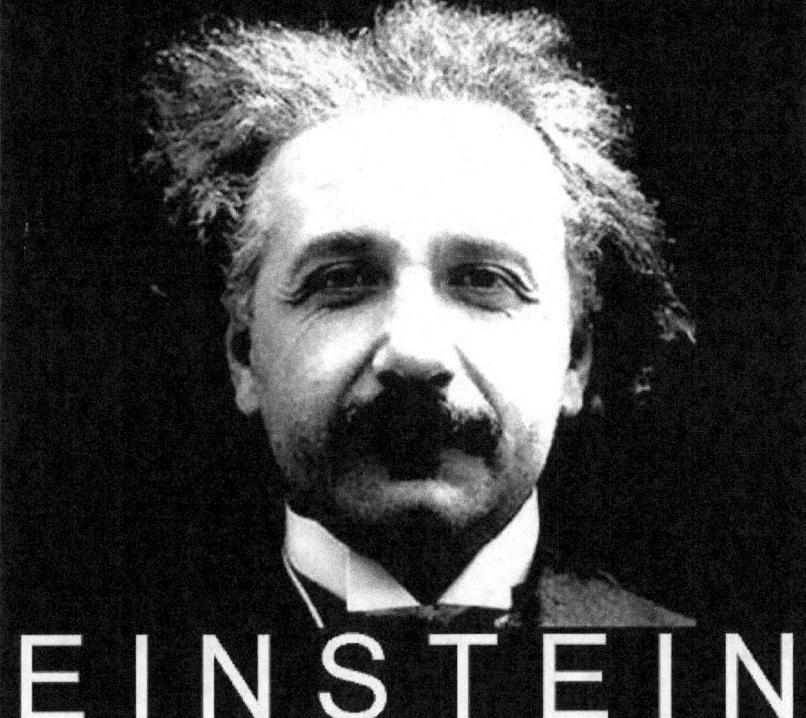

"I am convinced there is only *one* way to eliminate these grave evils, namely through the establishment of a socialist economy, accompanied by an educational system which would be oriented toward social goals. In such an economy, the means of production are owned by society itself and are utilized in a planned fashion. A planned economy, which adjusts production to the needs of the community, would distribute the work to be done among all those able to work and would guarantee a livelihood to every man, woman, and child."

EINSTEIN

Obviously Swindoll is wrong:

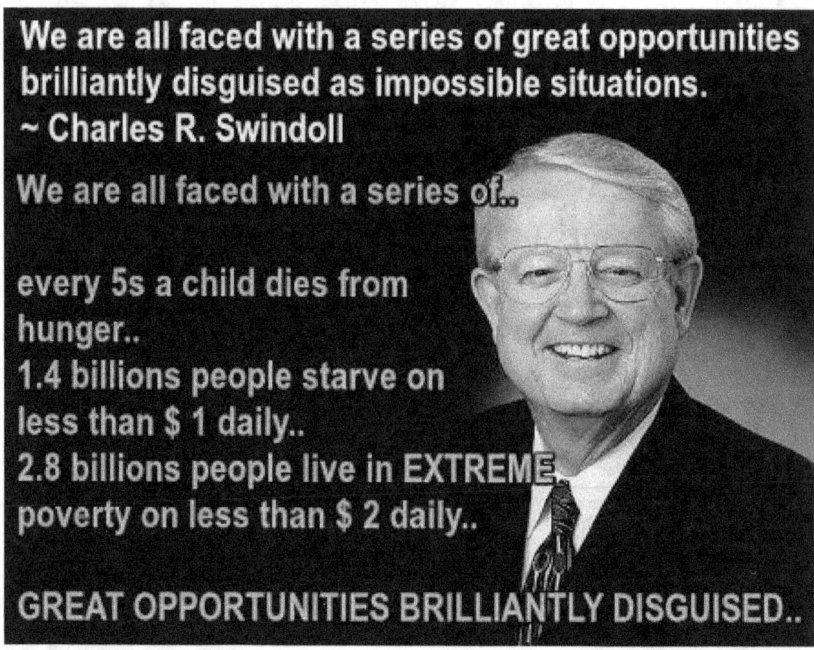

We are all faced with a series of great opportunities
brilliantly disguised as impossible situations.
~ Charles R. Swindoll

We are all faced with a series of...

every 5s a child dies from
hunger..
1.4 billions people starve on
less than $ 1 daily..
2.8 billions people live in EXTREME
poverty on less than $ 2 daily..

GREAT OPPORTUNITIES BRILLIANTLY DISGUISED..

WE
ARE THE ONES
WE'VE BEEN
WAITING FOR.

If you are waiting
for a sign from the
UNIVERSE
This is it!
Now go big.

This is how this whole planet – Global Village of one tribe which is the whole Humanity – should look and work like:

An anthropologist proposed a game to the kids in an African tribe. He put a basket full of fruit near a tree and told them that whoever got there first won the sweet fruits. When he gave them the signal to run they all took each other's hands and ran together, then sat in a circle enjoying their treats. When he asked them why they chose to run as a group when they could have had more fruit individually, one child spoke up and said: "UBUNTU, how can one of us be happy if all the other ones are sad?"

'UBUNTU' in the Xhosa culture means: "I am because we are"

When you are surrounded by people who share a passionate commitment around

a common purpose.. anything is possible..
~ Howard Schultz

~I am deliberate, and afraid of nothing~

6.The example of Canada in the background of the hypothetical English domination over the 15 countries nowadays "The commonwealth realm" and the whole world

Nowadays there are 15 countries considered "The commonwealth realm" including Canada, New Zealand, Australia and obviously the United Kingdom with Wales, Scotland and northern Ireland but there are also former Commonwealth countries like for instance India, South Africa Republic or Ireland. One interesting and significant fact about UK is that England took over and controls Scottish oil fields in the Northern Sea as well as they took over their gold mines.

It's Scotland's oil:

http://en.wikipedia.org/wiki/It%27s_Scotland%27s_oil

This would prove to me partially that Wales, Ireland and Scotland are still under the English occupation as well as New Zealand, Australia, South Africa, India, Canada AND USA [as simply the English vassal and barracks] and though officially they are not English colonies any more as they all once were but in fact England and the English queen AND the British House of Lords nominated by the queen solely and exclusively [not so seemingly powerless as well as apparently the queen whose role and function is NOT only official and representative]. Certainly the English socially-economically-political influences in the mentioned countries are not ZERO.

Besides the role and power of the English House of Lords may be highly underestimated. Officially The House of Commons has much greater power but the lords are often great authorities to the UK inhabitants and their opinions count a lot and thus they may influence the HoC to a huge degree.. just a hypothesis.. So how strong are they? You tell me.

The commonwealth realm:

http://en.wikipedia.org/wiki/Commonwealth_realm

The monarchy of Canada is the core of both Canada's federalism and its Westminster-style parliamentary democracy, being the foundation of the executive, legislative, and judicial branches of the Canadian government and each provincial government. The current Canadian monarch, since 6 February 1952, is Queen Elizabeth II. Although the person of the sovereign is equally shared with fifteen other independent countries within the Commonwealth of Nations, each country's monarchy is [ONLY OFFICIALLY!] separate and legally distinct.

The Senate of Canada (French: Sénat du Canada) is a component of the Parliament of Canada, along with the House of Commons, and the monarch (Queen of England represented by the governor general). The Senate is modelled after the British House of Lords and consists of 105 members appointed by the governor general on the advice of the prime minister.

The Queen lives predominantly in the United Kingdom and, while several powers are the sovereign's alone, most of the royal governmental and ceremonial duties in Canada are carried out by the Queen's representative, the governor general.

Per the Canadian constitution, the responsibilities of the sovereign and/or governor general include summoning and dismissing parliament, calling elections, and appointing governments. Further, Royal Assent and the royal sign-manual are required to enact laws, letters patent, and orders in council.

The Governor General of Canada [French [masculine]: Gouverneur général du Canada, or [feminine]: Gouverneure générale du Canada] is the federal viceregal representative of the Canadian monarch, currently Queen Elizabeth II. Because the person of the sovereign is shared equally both with the 15 other Commonwealth realms and the 10 provinces of Canada and resides predominantly in her oldest realm, the United Kingdom, she, on the advice of the Canadian prime minister, appoints the governor general to carry out most of her constitutional and ceremonial duties.

Canada's constitution is based on the Westminster parliamentary model, wherein the role of the Queen is both legal and practical, but not political.

The government of Canada – formally termed Her Majesty's Government – is defined by the constitution as the Queen acting on the advice of her Privy Council; what is technically known as the Queen-in-Council, or sometimes the Governor-in-Council, referring to the governor general as the Queen's stand-in. One of the main duties of the Crown is to "ensure that a democratically elected government is always in place," which means appointing a prime minister to thereafter head the Cabinet – a committee of the Privy Council charged with advising the Crown on the exercise of the royal prerogative. The Queen is informed by her viceroy of the swearing-in and resignation of prime ministers and other members of the ministry, remains fully briefed through regular communications from her Canadian ministers, and holds audience with them whenever possible. Per convention, the content of these communications and meetings remains confidential, so as to protect the impartiality of the monarch and her representative. The appropriateness and viability of this tradition in an age of social media has been questioned.

English House of Lords [2010–present]

The Conservative–Liberal Democrat coalition agreed, following the 2010 general election, to clearly outline a provision for a wholly or mainly elected second chamber, elected by a proportional representation system. These proposals sparked a debate on 29 June 2010. As an interim measure, appointment of new peers will reflect shares of the vote secured by the political parties in the last general election.

Detailed proposals for Lords reform including a draft House of Lords Reform Bill were published on 17 May 2011. These include a 300-member hybrid house, of which 80% are elected. A further 20% would be appointed, and reserve space would be included for some Church of England bishops. Under the proposals, members would also serve single non-renewable terms of 15 years. Former Mps would be allowed to stand for election to the Upper House, but members of the Upper House would not be immediately allowed to become Mps.

The details of the proposal were:

The upper chamber shall continue to be known as the House of Lords for legislative purposes.

The reformed House of Lords should have 300 members of which 240 are "Elected Members" and 60 appointed "Independent Members". Up to 12 Church of England bishops may sit in the house as ex-officio "Lords Spiritual".

Elected Members will serve a single, non renewable term of 15 years.

Elections to the reformed Lords should take place at the same time as elections to the House of Commons.

Elected Members should be elected using the Single Transferable Vote system of proportional representation.

Twenty Independent Members [a third] shall take their seats within the reformed house at the same time as elected members do so and for the same 15-year term.

Independent Members will be appointed by the Queen after being suggested by the Prime Minister acting on advice of an Appointments Commission.

There will no longer be a link between the peerage system and membership of the upper house.

The current powers of the House of Lords would not change and the House of Commons shall retain its status as the primary House of Parliament.

The proposals were considered by a Joint Committee on House of Lords Reform made up of both Mps and Peers, which issued its final report on 23 April 2012, making the following suggestions:

The reformed House of Lords should have 450 members.

Party groupings, including the Crossbenchers, should

choose which of their members are retained in the transition period, with the percentage of members allotted to each group based on their share of the peers with high attendance during a given period.

Up to 12 Lords Spiritual should be retained in a reformed House of Lords.

Relationship with the Government

The House of Lords does not control the term of the Prime Minister or of the Government. Only the Lower House may force the Prime Minister to resign or call elections by passing a motion of no-confidence or by withdrawing supply. Thus, the House of Lords' oversight of the government is limited.

Most Cabinet ministers are from the House of Commons rather than the House of Lords. In particular, all Prime Ministers since 1902 have been members of the Lower House.[Alec Douglas-Home, who became Prime Minister in 1963 whilst still an Earl, disclaimed his peerage and was elected to the Commons soon after his term began.] In recent history, it has been very rare for major cabinet positions [except Lord Chancellor and Leader of the House of Lords] to have been filled by peers.

Exceptions include Lord Carrington, who was the Foreign Secretary between 1979 and 1982, Lord Young of Graffham [Minister without Portfolio, then Secretary of State for Employment and then Secretary of State for Trade and Industry from 1984 to 1989], and Lord Mandelson, who served as First Secretary of State, Secretary of State for Business, Innovation and Skills and

President of the Board of Trade. George Robertson was briefly a peer whilst serving as Secretary of State for Defense before resigning to take up the post of Secretary General of NATO. From 1999 to 2010 the Attorney General for England and Wales was a Member of the House of Lords; the most recent was Baroness Scotland of Asthal.

The House of Lords remains a source for junior ministers and members of government. Like the House of Commons, the Lords also has a Government Chief Whip as well as several Junior Whips. Where a government department is not represented by a minister in the Lords or one is not available, government whips will act as spokesmen for them.

How members are appointed [by the English Queen]:

http://www.parliament.uk/business/lords/whos-in-the-house-of-lords/members-and-their-roles/how-members-are-appointed/

7. Addendum: The Egyptian variant..

I am thinking about the rule of the world by Contemporary lines of ancient Egyptian priests – some may be not of this planet – Egypt was apparently defeated by Rome but by Rome which applied some Egyptian systems and assimilated many Egyptians socially high and that influenced the whole Europe under Rome at those times and I want to write how this refers to the modern world..

Germany also lost the war like Egypt but they had been stealing and robbing allover the world for 8 years (I and II WW) and are so forward on these wars, as indeed you can see – thanks to "losing wars" have dominated for some 40 years in Europe right now and militarily as well..

..so maybe we in fact are still living in the pharaohs'
147

Egypt steered and ruled by the successors of the most powerful Egyptian priesthood caste..

This is just such a pre-planned matrix, but before that I need to get acquainted with history, and mythology of Egypt – already started and just as Rome – once Europe was also within Rome and UK [the Celts and Galls lands] included so probably I will add some druids and Stonehenge stuff, the oldest royal lines and aristocratic dynasties of the financial magnates such as Rockefeller, De Beer, Warburg, Hapsburg, Mellon, Vanderbilt..

..and of course Rothschild Dynasty – the family is large and maybe controlled this planet together with the Egyptian priests of Vatican – and one of them bought a 18th century central point in the world bank – the Bank of England – the main bank of the ENGLISH NOT British Empire of which parts are USA, AU, CAN, NZ and the European Union and United Nations – based in New York - England and its vassal USA founded the Ligue of Nations in 1918 and later transformed it into UN with HQ in NYC.. imho USA is just English barracks.. Plus the '"former"' Commonwealth aspect.. Just an idea for one of my next books.. any cooperation welcome gladly..

8. Some of my favorite quotes I found in the Web which inspire me greatly and which I do consider true. Some still under question..

..like a few quotes of myself for instance ;) :D Yes. I DO quote myself! Why in the hell NOT?

We have now sunk to a depth at which restatement of the obvious is the first duty of intelligent men. ~ George Orwell

Choose a path that stimulates your mind and invigorates your soul. ~ Dan Goldberg

Nobody can teach you Love. Love you have to find yourself, within your being, by rising your consciousness to higher levels. ~ Osho

Courage is the Love Affair with the Unknown. ~ Osho

Life [=Love ~ I] begins where Fear ends. ~ Osho

Live = Love and without real, true Love there is no True Life..True Love = Awakening = Life = Light = Wisdom = Courage = Compassion = Freedom = Equity = Truth = Honesty = Respect = Etc..

Love is Energy. Love is the key to Live. Without Love you are not aLive.. you are asleep.. zombie.. and Fear is the

antagonist of Love.. there is no Love where is Fear..
there is no Fear where is Love.. they exclude each other..

True Love = True Wisdom&Kindness = True Life.. True
Love = True Awakening sought by so many.. just as
simple.. ~ I

You don't love someone because of their looks or their
clothes or their car.. you love them because they sing a
song only your heart can understand.. ~ Web

Physical attractions are common but a mental connection
is rare.. once you've had the latter, the former will never
be enough again.. ~ Web

When you meet the other half of your soul, you will
understand why all the others let you go.. when you meet
the one who deserves your heart, you'll understand why
things didn't work out with everyone else.. ~ Web

When you find the one that connects with your soul and
your love is meant to be.. your spirit will feel free and sing
a sweet song that will encourage you and make you
strong.. the right one in your life will make you proud of
who you are and who you have become.. and nothing will
tear you apart.. ~ Web

All love that has not friendship for its base is like a
mansion built upon the sand.. ~ Web

Vibrate at the highest possible frequency. ~ Web

The real question is not whether life exists after death. The real question is whether you are alive before death. ~ Osho

Truth is available only to those who have the courage to question whatever they have been taught.. ~ Unknown

Unthinking respect for authority is the greatest enemy of Truth.. ~ Einstein

Question everything generally thought to be obvious.. ~ Dieter Rams

There are only two mistakes one can make along the road to truth: not going all the way, and not starting.. - Buddha

In order to be effective Truth must penetrate like an arrow.. and that is likely to hurt.. ~ Wei Wu Wei

That which can be destroyed by the Truth should be.. ~ P.C. Hodgell, C. Sagan

Truth is by nature self-evident. As soon as you remove the cobwebs of ignorance that surround it, it shines clear. - Gandhi

In a time of universal deceit – telling the truth is a

revolutionary act.. ~ George Orwell

When a well-packaged web of lies has been sold gradually to the masses over generations, the Truth will seem utterly preposterous and its speaker a RAVING LUNATIC. ~ D. James

Those who are able to see beyond the shadows and lies of their culture will never be understood, let alone believed, by the masses.. ~ Plato

Political language... is designed to make lies sound truthful and murder respectable, and to give an appearance of solidity to pure wind.. ~ George Orwell

The very concept of objective truth is fading out of the world. Lies will pass into history.. ~ George Orwell

If we never know truth then we never know love. If we know truth and not act upon it, then what is real love all about?

All truths are easy to understand once they are discovered; the point is to discover them.. ~ Galileo

The truth is incontrovertible; malice may attack it, ignorance may deride it, but in the end, there it is.. ~ Winston Churchill

Pretty words are not always true and true words are not always pretty. ~ Web

Never assume the obvious is true. - W. Saffire

The mind is like a parachute, it doesn't work unless its OPEN ~ Dalai Lama

A closed mind is like a closed book: just a block of wood. - Chinese Proverb

OPEN MINDS Sees Truth Everywhere! Love Your Self. Love the Truth.

Whatever is good for your soul – DO THAT! ~ Web

Don't ask what the world needs. Ask what makes you come alive and go do it. Because what world needs is people who have come alive. ~ Howard Truman

To make the right choices in life, you have to get in touch with your soul. To do this, you need to experience solitude, which most people are afraid of, because in the silence you hear the truth and know the solutions. ~ Deepak Chopra

Ultimately spiritual awareness unfolds when you are flexible, when you are spontaneous, when you are detached, when you are easy on yourself and easy on others [just don't overdose "easy" ;) ~ I]. ~ Deepak Chopra

153

Assume NOTHING. Question EVERYTHING. - Charles
Patterson

Wisdom begins in wonder ~ Socrates

The cure for ignorance is to QUESTION. ~ prophet
Mohammed

Simplicity is the ultimate sophistication. ~ L. da Vinci

If you are depressed you are living in the past.

If you are anxious you are living in the future.

If you are at peace you are living in the P R E S E N T. ~
Lao Tzu

Purify your eyes, and see the pure world. Your life will fill
with radiant forms. ~ Rumi

Energy goes where attention flows. What's your attention
focused on? ~ Web

Words and thoughts are Energy. Use them wisely. ~ Web

Nothing has changed. Except my attitude. Therefore
everything has changed. ~ Anthony de Mello

Exponentially shrinking numbers of increasingly
enlightened people are deemed insane by exponentially
increasing masses of decreasingly enlightened people. ~

xlivescom

Go to work, send your kids to school, follow fashion, act normal, walk on the pavement, watch TV, save for your old age, obey the law, repeat after me: I AM FREE!

Untrain yourself of fear. Once you learn to do this then will you understand what it really means to be free. You were born free. Now live. ~ Web

If you have fear of some pain or suffering, you should examine whether there is anything you can do about it. If you can, there is no need to worry about it; if you cannot do anything, then there is also no need to worry. ~ Dalai Lama

I will not let anyone walk through my mind with their dirty feet. ~ Gandhi

Any fool can know, the point is to understand. ~ Albert Einstein

Question EVERYTHING. ~ Albert Einstein

Assume nothing. Fear nothing. Question everything. Open your eyes. Challenge the opposition. And start thinking for yourself ~ Web

Do not believe in anything simply because you have heard it. Do not believe in traditions because they have been handed down for many generations. Do not believe anything because it is spoken and rumored by many. Do not believe in anything because it is written in your religious books. Do not believe in anything merely on the authority of your teachers and elders. But after observation and analysis, when you find that anything agrees with reason and is conducive to the good and the benefit of one and all, then accept it and live up to it. ~ Buddha

They'll call me crazy until they find out I'm right. ~ Web

Question everything generally thought to be obvious. ~ Dieter Rams

Unthinking respect for authority is the greatest enemy of Truth. ~ A. Einstein

The whole problem with the world is that fools and fanatics are so certain of themselves and wiser people so full of doubts. ~ Bertrand Russel, Charles Bukowski

To argue with a person who has renounced the use of reason is like administering medicine to the dead. ~ Paine

It is difficult to free the fools from the chains they revere. ~ Voltaire

Intelligence without wisdom brings destruction. ~ E. Ozan

The world will not be destroyed by those who do Evil but by those who WATCH them without doing ANYTHING. ~ A. Einstein

I The world is in greater peril from those who tolerate or encourage evil than from those who actually commit it..

II The world is a dangerous place not because of those who do Evil, but because of those who look on and do nothing.. ~ Einstein

Without Justice there can be no Peace.. he who passively accepts Evil is as much involved in it as he who helps to perpetrate it.. he who accepts Evil without protesting against it is really cooperating with it.. ~ MLK

The function of Wisdom is to discriminate between Good and Evil.. ~ Marcus Tulius Cicero

The battle-line between Good and Evil runs through the heart of every man.. ~ Aleksandr Solzhenitsyn

All tyranny needs to gain a foothold is for people of good conscience to remain silent.. ~ T. Jefferson

All that is necessary for the triumph of Evil is for good men to do nothing.. ~ Edmund Burke

Poverty is the WORST form of violence [..and therefore it is Evil, too].. ~ Gandhi

Strong people stand up for themselves but the strongest people stand up for others. ~ Web

You do not need a reason to help people. ~ Web

You are not a sheep. Stop acting like one. ~ Web

I always wandered why didn't somebody do something about that. Then I realized I am Somebody. ~ Web

Keep calm and carry on? No thanks. I'd rather rise hell and change the world. ~ Web

People who say it cannot be done should not interrupt those who ARE doing it. ~ Web

Start where you are. Use what you have. Do what you can. ~ A. Ashe

A year from now you may wish you had started today. ~ K. Lamb

Let nothing enslave you. ~ Web

The closer you get to excellence in your life, the more friends you'll lose..

People love you when you're average because it makes them comfortable..

But when you pursue greatness it makes people uncomfortable..

Be prepared to lose some people on your journey.. ~ Tony A. Gaskins Jr.

You have permission to walk away from anything that doesn't feel right..

Trust your instinct and listen to your inner voice ~ it's trying to protect you.. ~ Bryant McGill

Cutting people off my life does not mean I hate them.. it simply means I respect me.. not everyone is meant to stay.. ~ Web

When you are surrounded by people who share a passionate commitment around a common purpose.. anything is possible.. ~ Howard Schultz

I am realistic: I expect miracles. ~ W. Dyer

Change is the essence of Life. ~ Web

NOTHING is IMPOSSIBLE. Some things are just less likely than others. ~ J. Winters

Take the attitude of a student – never be too big to ask questions, never know too much to learn something new. - Og Mandino

Once you stop learning you start dying. - Albert Einstein

The important thing is not to stop questioning. - Albert Einstein

Sword is not meant to kill. It is meant to protect the most precious [that which matters most]. ~ I&Seraph

In a time of universal deceit – telling the truth is a revolutionary act. ~ George Orwell

The great enemy of clear language is insincerity. When there is a gap between one's real and one's declared aims, one turns, as it were, instinctively to long words and exhausted idioms, like a cuttlefish squirting out ink. ~ George Orwell

On the whole, human beings want to be good, but not too good, and not quite all the time. ~ George Orwell

Political language... is designed to make lies sound truthful and murder respectable, and to give an appearance of solidity to pure wind. ~ George Orwell

Myths which are believed in tend to become true. ~ George Orwell

Nowadays truly good men must not pledge loyalty to their country, nation, religion, government or political party because it would eventually negate and compromise their kindness. ~ I

1 MU57 N¤7 F34R

F34R 15 7H3 M1ND-K1LL3R.

F34R 15 7H3 L177L3-D347H 7H47 8R1N65 7¤74L ¤8L173R471¤N.

1 W1LL F4C3 MY F34R.

1 W1LL P3RM17 I7 7¤ P455 ¤V3R M3 4ND 7HR¤UGH M3.

4ND WH3N 17 H45 6¤N3 P457 1 W1LL 7URN 7H3 1NN3R 3Y3 7¤ 533 175 P47H.

WH3R3 7H3 F34R H45 G¤N3 7H3R3 W1LL B3 N¤7H1N6.

¤NLY 1 W1LL R3M41N.

Live totally and live intensely so that each moment becomes golden and your whole life becomes a series of golden moments. ~ Osho

War against a foreign country only happens when the moneyed classes think they are going to profit from it. ~ George Orwell

Who controls the past controls the future. Who controls the present controls the past. ~ George Orwell

In our age there is no such thing as 'keeping out of politics.' All issues are political issues, and politics itself is a mass of lies, evasions, folly, hatred and schizophrenia. ~ George Orwell

Forgiveness is the key to Love which matters most. You must forgive everyone including yourself any harm done to anyone including yourself. This will free your heart and mind from many [all?] negative feelings, emotions or thoughts accompanying them and associated with Fear which block you from Love and Awakening and will shift you up in a lightning manner.. a quickening.. it works.. I did it and I know others who did.. <3 :)

The most effective first step for the lightning evolution of mind is to question and reject for the time being EVERYTHING you know at once. After that you should build your own knowledge anew based ONLY on what you know for sure (true or false) ~ there will be not much of it – and the rest are merely possibilities – many of which are falsehood when seen as facts. In effect your mind will be free of false convictions and thus open for the real Truth. And the part of it is that MOST things are BUT possibilities. Lastly, always be ready to question ANYTHING you know because "Change Is the Essence of Life". ~ I

For the above, namely opening for the Truth, it is essential that you are true ~ that the Truth is within you. Among other things this means that you should ALWAYS speak Truth and never lie. This is a question of strong, inner decision to speak only Truth and this will take some time.. firstly you must know what the Truth is.. then you will be able to tell the Truth from lies.. in the end you will just sense it straight away.. ~ I

We should see and do things using the Fusion of Heart and Mind. None of the two must be undervalued. We should think~feel by means of this Fusion. Neither Heart nor Mind is most important for our correct perception – delivering the real, full picture, its correct analysis, consequent decisions and actions. They BOTH must closely collaborate together to achieve that. ~ I

Imho the vast majority of people mistake knowledge and/or intelligence or just being smart for Wisdom.

I do not care how many wise or "wise" books u read nor how many youtube movies you saw.. one can read 50 000 books and still remain stupid.. books bring knowledge and not directly wisdom and knowledge and/or intelligence do not imply wisdom. Wise in my terms is Good= living a loveful life..

Knowledge and intelligence are merely tools and like a knife, a hammer or an ax in the hands of a stupid=bad man are a curse to the world and in hands of a good=wise man are a blessing. ~ I

The mind is like an umbrella, it works better when it is open ~ Zuli Masih

I know that I am intelligent, because I know that I know nothing. ~ Socrates

The only true wisdom is in knowing you know nothing.. ~ Socrates

If you want to awaken all of humanity, then awaken all of yourself. If you want to eliminate the suffering in the world, then eliminate all that is dark and negative in yourself. Truly, the greatest gift you have to give is that of your own self-transformation. [and AFTER you are DONE with THAT – DO CHANGE THE WORLD – I] ~ Lao Tzu

You should respect each other and refrain from disputes; you should not, like water and oil, repel each other, but should, like milk and water, mingle together. ~ Zuli Masih

Concentrate on your inner world. That is where your heaven and hell are created. ~ Philip Arnold

No colour, no religion, no nationality should come between us. We are all children of God. ~ Mother Teresa

I believe in the fundamental truth of all great religions of the world. — Mahatma Gandhi

Until there is peace between religions, there can be no peace in the world. ~ Thich Nhat Hanh

Yoga teaches us to cure what need not be endured and endure what cannot be cured. ~ B.K.S. Iyengar

A realized soul is like a river or a tree, giving comfort and coolness to those who come to him.

Where there is love, there is no effort. ~ Amma

A generous heart, kind speech, and a life of service and

compassion are the things which renew humanity. ~ The
Buddha

Realize that everything connects to everything else. ~
Leonardo DaVinci?

Creating without claiming, Doing without taking credit,
Guiding without interfering, This is Primal Virtue. ~ Lao
Tzu

Truth is the daughter of inspiration.. Intellectual analysis
and partialized debate keep the people away from the
truth..It is like a finger pointing a way to the moon. Do not
concentrate on the finger or you will miss all that
heavenly glory ~ Bruce Lee

Great spirits have always encountered violent opposition
from mediocre minds. ~ Albert Einstein

The world is my country, all mankind are my brethren,
and to do good is my religion. ~ Thomas Paine

People take different roads seeking fulfillment and
happiness. Just because they're not on your road, does
not mean they have gotten lost. ~ Dalai Lama

Kindness in words creates confidence. Kindness in
thinking creates profoundness. Kindness in giving
creates love. ~ Lao Tzu

Be a lamp, a lifeboat, a ladder. Help someone's soul heal.

Walk out of your house like a shepherd. ~ Mevlana Rumi (1207 – 1273)

Prayer is when you talk to God; meditation is when you listen to God. ~ Diana Robinson

Kindness is the language which the deaf can hear and the blind can see. ~ Mark Twain

Be a light unto yourself. Be your own confidence. Hold to the truth within.~ Buddha

Your vision will become clear only when you look into your heart. Who looks outside, dreams. Who looks inside, awakens. ~ Carl Jung

Look within, for within is the wellspring of virtue, which will not cease flowing, if you cease not from digging. ~ Marcus Aurelius

Be more concerned with your character than with your reputation. Your character is what you really are while your reputation is merely what others think you are. ~ Dale Carnegie

A generous heart, kind speech, and a life of service and compassion are the things which renew humanity. ~ The Buddha

To keep the body in good health is a duty... otherwise we shall not be able to keep our mind strong and clear. ~

Buddha

A human being is part of a whole, called by us the "Universe" a part limited in time and space.

He experiences himself, his thoughts and feelings, as something separated from the rest--a kind of optical delusion of his consciousness. This delusion is a kind of prison for us, restricting us to our personal desires and to affection for a few persons nearest us.

Our task must be to free ourselves from this prison by widening our circles of compassion to embrace all living creatures and the whole of nature in its beauty. ~ Albert Einstein

When man destroys nature, man is actually destroying himself." ~ Rachel Carson

People don't care how much you know, until they know how much you care...for them..

Sometimes the smallest things take up the most room in your heart. ~ Winnie the Pooh

Believe nothing, no matter where you read it, or who has said it, not even if I have said it, unless it agrees with your own reason and your own common sense. ~ Buddha

Easy vs Difficult" "Easy is to judge the Mistakes of others" "Difficult is to Recognize our own Mistakes" "Easy is to Hurt Someone who Loves you" "Difficult is to Heal the

Wound" "Easy is to set Rules.." "Difficult is to follow them" "Easy is to Dream Every Night" "Difficult is to Fight For a Dream" "Easy is to say we Love" "Difficult is to show it Every day" "Easy is to make Mistakes" "Difficult is to Learn From Them" ~ Unknown.

Heroism on command, senseless violence, and all the loathsome nonsense that goes by the name of patriotism – how passionately I hate them! ~ Albert Einstein

Patriotism is as fierce as a fever, pitiless as the grave, blind as a stone, and irrational as a headless hen. ~ Ambrose Bierce

Patriotism varies, from a noble devotion to a moral lunacy. ~ W. R. Inge

A patriot must always be ready to defend his country against his government. ~ Edward Abbey

The duty of a patriot is to protect his country from its government. ~ Thomas Paine

To oppose corruption in government is the highest obligation of patriotism. ~ G. Edward Griffin

Patriotism is the virtue of the vicious. ~ Oscar Wilde

The love of one's country is a splendid thing. But why should love stop at the border? ~ Pablo Casals

You're not supposed to be so blind with patriotism that you can't face reality. Wrong is wrong, no matter who says it. ~ Malcolm X

When a whole nation is roaring Patriotism at the top of its voice, I am fain to explore the cleanness of its hands and purity of its heart. ~ Ralph Waldo Emerson

Patriotism is a pernicious, psychopathic form of idiocy. ~ George Bernard Shaw

Patriotism is usually stronger than class hatred, and always stronger than internationalism. ~ George Orwell

A set of few prophetic quotations by a genius writer George Orwell (1903-1950):

The nationalist not only does not disapprove of atrocities committed by his own side, but he has a remarkable capacity for not even hearing about them.

The very concept of objective truth is fading out of the world. Lies will pass into history.

War is a way of shattering to pieces... materials which might otherwise be used to make the masses too comfortable and... too intelligent.

No advance in wealth, no softening of manners, no reform or revolution has ever brought human equality a millimeter nearer.

We have now sunk to a depth at which restatement of the obvious is the first duty of intelligent men.

Progress is not an illusion, it happens, but it is slow and invariably disappointing.

In our time political speech and writing are largely the defense of the indefensible.

If you want a vision of the future, imagine a boot stamping on a human face – forever.

Power is not a means, it is an end.

Only after the last tree's cut, And the last river poisoned; Only after the last fish is caught, Will you find that money cannot be eaten. ~ Some Indians

Every man must decide whether he will walk in the light of creative altruism or in the darkness of destructive selfishness ~ MLK

Only the open mind can be ready to listen to something that goes against it. The closed mind can listen only to that which supports it. ~ OSHO

There is almost a sensual longing for communion with others who have a large vision. The immense fulfillment of the friendship between those engaged in furthering the evolution of consciousness has a quality impossible to describe. ~ Pierre Teilhard de Chardin.

The world is round so that friendship may encircle it. ~ Pierre Teilhard de Chardin.

Don't gain the world and lose your soul, wisdom is better than silver or gold. - Bob Marley

Get up, stand up, Stand up for your rights. Get up, stand up, Don't give up the fight. ~ Bob Marley

NOW THIS IS NOT THE END. IT IS NOT EVEN THE BEGINNING OF THE END. BUT IT IS, PERHAPS, THE END OF THE BEGINNING.

THIS IS NOT THE END

BUT I CAN SEE IT FROM HERE

We are here to generate the Lightning Evolution: rEvolution unlike any that has gone before: the TSUNAMI of Awakened and Aware Consciousness which will sweep the planet and shake our modern world to its very core..

If you like my work then you may wish to donate me even a smallest sum if you can. For the donation options and forum I invite you to my website meant for this book and there is more stuff you may like there:

http://lightningevolution.wix.com/humanity-evolution

DISCLAIMER: Except for 2 graphics none [including mine] are copyrighted. I could not locate and contact the author of AAs Michael and Raphael [Mr/Ms Waters] - I offer 0.55% of my total sale for AA Raphael and 1.18% for AA Michael [I love it O:) <3] - total 1.73%..

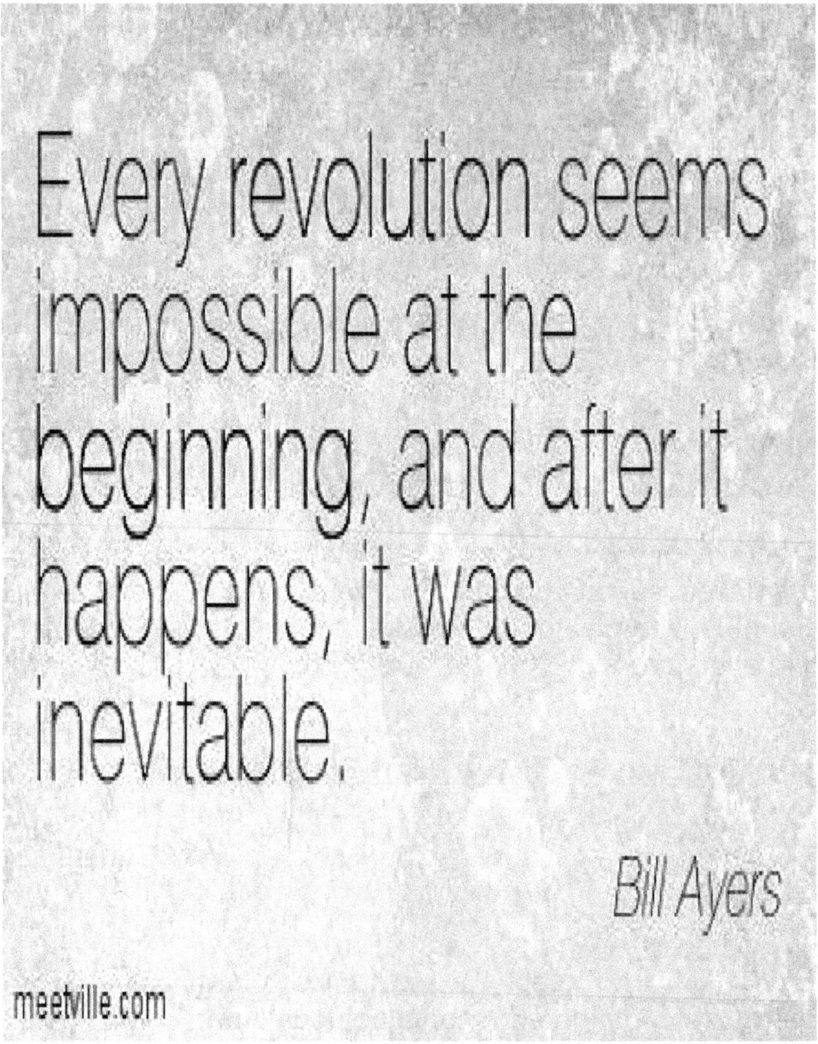

Every revolution seems
impossible at the
beginning, and after it
happens, it was
inevitable.

Bill Ayers

at first glance it may appear too hard. look again. always look again.

Whhaad White Dragon: I was born in 1969 and I am a Leo. I live in a small out of the grid village in Western Poland.. The youngsters here and not only them call me Jedi.. :D A vast fertile forest with swamps begins right outside my gate and I have 20mins walk to a very clean lake.. I am a spiritual holistic healer and shaman, truthseeker and Truthsayer, philosopher, thinker, writer, mathematician, martial artist, pathfinder and wayshower and more.. most probably Arcturian seed.. I got the maximum result in the Mensa entry test: IQ156 and never had any urge to take another test to measure how much higher my IQ actually possibly was.. I guess I speak telepathically/energetically with two dragons spotted near me, with gods, angels, stars, planets, animals and plants.. and some people.. And there is more.. O:)

www.ingramcontent.com/pod-product-compliance
Lightning Source LLC
Chambersburg PA
CBHW070354290526
45790CB00004B/1489

* 9 7 8 1 5 0 3 1 7 5 0 2 0 *